MW00456359

Inspiration
from the
Saints

INSPIRATION
from the
SAINTS

✳ ✳ ✳

Stories from the Lives of
Catholic Holy Men and Women

MAOLSHEACHLANN
Ó CEALLAIGH

Angelico Press

First published in the USA
by Angelico Press 2018
Copyright © 2018 Maolsheachlann Ó Ceallaigh

For information, address:
Angelico Press, Ltd.
169 Monitor St.
Brooklyn, NY 11222
www.angelicopress.com

978-1-62138-335-2 ppr
978-1-62138-336-9 cloth
978-1-62138-337-6 ebook

Book and cover design
by Michael Schrauzer

This book is dedicated
to my beloved wife Michelle.

When I see your face,
what I am looking at is home.

Acknowledgements

FIRST OF ALL, I WOULD LIKE TO THANK MY BEAUTIFUL wife Michelle, my muse and inspiration in this project as in all things.

Secondly, I'd like to thank all my family for their help during the writing of this book, especially my father, who has always encouraged my writing.

Thanks to the readers of my blog *Irish Papist* for all their suggestions for the book, and for their continued interest in my writing. Thanks also to Jonathan Barry and the other members of the Gothic Club, whose literary and artistic achievements have galvanized my own efforts. I look forward to many more slices of lemon drizzle cake, and many more discussions of great horror films and books.

My friend Roger Buck contributed an incredible amount of time and attention to this project. I cannot thank him enough. I'm also indebted to Daniel Conneally for his interest and support, to Fr. Donncha Ó hAodha for his encouragement and help, and to Fr. Paul Stenhouse for his eagle eye and suggestions.

The bulk of the research for this book was done in the Central Catholic Library, Dublin. Therefore I must thank all the staff and volunteers who make this unique resource available in the face of so many challenges.

Thanks to the following individuals and companies for kindly allowing me permission to quote material:

Glen Dallaire of the St. Gemma Galgani website.

Darragh Redin of Veritas Publications.

Libreria Editrice Vaticana, for various ecclesial documents.

Fr. Paul Spencer CP for the photograph of St. Charles of Mount Argus.

Thanks to ICS Publications for quotations from *Story of a Soul*, translated by John Clarke, O.C.D. Copyright (c) 1975, 1976, 1996 by Washington Province of Discalced Carmelites, ICS Publications, 2131

Lincoln Road, N.E. Washington, DC 20002-1199 U.S.A. www.icspublications.org

Thanks to the Catholic Truth Society for Mary Craig's passage on Maximilian Kolbe, whose original source is *Blessed Maximilian Kolbe, Priest Hero of a Death Camp*, Mary Craig, Catholic Truth Society, London, 1973.

Thanks to The Word Among Us, 7115 Guilford Dr. #100, Frederick, MD 21704, for quotations from Mitch Finley's *The Rosary Handbook: A Guide for Newcomers, Old-Timers and Those in Between*.

Lastly, I must thank the subject of this book — the saints themselves. I ask them to pray for me, for everyone listed in these acknowledgments, and for everybody who reads this book!

Contents

Introduction

FOR MOST OF MY LIFE I DIDN'T CARE VERY MUCH about the saints. In fact, it would be truer to say that I didn't care about them at all.

Long before I realized that the first day of November was All Saints' Day—the day that Catholics (and many other Christians) honor all the saints, including the countless saints who have never officially been proclaimed as such—I was much more excited about the evening that came before it: Halloween. I loved horror movies and spookiness and ghost stories. I still do. The lives of the saints, insofar as I was aware of them at all, seemed unspeakably dull.

It took me a long time to realize that *the very same thing that drew me* to horror movies and spooky stories could be found, in a much greater concentration, in the lives of the Catholic saints. In fact, it was this same quality that drew me to nearly everything that ever excited me.

What was this quality that drew me so? *Otherworldliness* is the best word I can think of to describe it—although "intensity," "transfiguration," "purity," and many other words also apply.

This is a book about Catholic saints, a book intended to inspire the reader with their stories and their words. But, since it's a very personal book, I want to first describe my own journey from a complete lack of interest in the saints to a deep fascination with them. And, strange as it might sound, I think that a comparison between All Saints' Day and Halloween, in terms of what they have meant to me through my life, may be the best way to do this.

As most people know, the full name of Halloween is "The Eve of All Hallows," and "All Hallows" is another name for "All Saints' Day." I grew up in Ireland, where I still live. Halloween, with all its monster masks, bonfires and fireworks, was a big deal in Ireland. Indeed, I didn't realize until relatively recently that the celebration had its roots in my own country, in the pagan festival of Samhain (pronounced sow-wan).

1

Samhain was a harvest festival, and a time when the boundary between the world of the living and the dead was supposed to become particularly thin — a time when the dead might be expected to wander into the world of the living.

The idea that All Saints' Day was invented to "replace" Samhain is just a myth — indeed, there was a time when All Saints' Day was celebrated on the 13th of May. The relationship between the two days, and exactly how and why All Saints' Day came to be celebrated on November 1st, is rather obscure. One way or another, the ancient pagan festival had borrowed its name from the Christian festival — but, in the popular mind (and certainly in my own mind), All Hallows was completely overshadowed by Halloween.

One particular Halloween party that I attended when I was a little boy had a profound, lifelong effect on me — perhaps nothing in my entire life has ever had a bigger effect. It was quite a modest party, mostly full of children but with a good sprinkling of adults too. All the usual trappings of a Halloween party were present — fruit, nuts, sweets, and the curranty cake that the Irish call *barmbrack*. I remember some kids playing bob-the-apple, the game in which players try to catch an apple in a basin of water with their teeth. Most of the children were "dressed up" (which is the Irish term for fancy dress) in various costumes — I must have been too, though I don't remember what I was "dressed up" as.

Outside, the evening air crackled with fireworks. I remember listening to some older boys discussing the various fireworks on display. It pleased me that there were actually different kinds of firework and that they had names. The firework whose name seemed most exotic to me, and which stirred my childish imagination in a way I can still vividly remember, was the "Catherine's wheel." It would be many, many years before I realized that it was named after a saint — St. Catherine of Alexandria, who was condemned to be martyred on an instrument called a spinning wheel (which broke up when she touched it — not that this saved her, since she was then simply beheaded).

The thing that enthralled me was that this evening was so *different*. It was *special*. The suburb I lived in had been transformed — it seemed like a different place entirely. From that night on, I craved that same kind of *specialness* with an almighty craving. I yearned for special times and special places. Just as Halloween was all about spookiness, and Christmas was all about merry-making, I wanted everything to be *all about something*. I wanted atmosphere and distinctiveness and character. The situations I relished the most were those which seemed most special, most atmospheric.

My first visit to the cinema was a good example. My parents took me and my brothers to see *Indiana Jones and the Temple of Doom*. I wanted to see *Star Trek: The Search for Spock*, but I was told I wouldn't like it. (I still regret this decision.) The dark, cavernous cinema, whose stuccoed ceilings and fancy upholstery seemed more elegant than anything I had ever seen before, was a world of its own — a world of drama, high emotion, and suspense.

Other settings also gratified this yearning for specialness. The beach. The museum. The circus. The exotic glamour of my local Chinese restaurant. And whenever there was a decent snowfall (in the Ireland of the eighties, such occasions were all too rare), the whole city became a new and magical place.

Of course, most of life wasn't like this. Most of life was neither one thing nor the other — ordinary days filled with homework and routine, weather that was neither wintery nor summery, rooms and halls and streets that had no particular character of their own…no *specialness*. And, oh, how that depressed me!

It wasn't just places and times that I wanted to be special, and different, and full of character. I wanted the same thing to be true about people. In fact, I assumed that it was true about people, and my slow realization that this was not the case caused me no small amount of anguish. Children think that adults have all the answers. I certainly did. I may not have assumed that adults have all the *right* answers — after all, I couldn't help noticing that they disagreed, so I knew they couldn't *all* be right — but I expected they all had *some* kind of answers, right or wrong. I thought that every grown-up had a fully-worked-out theory of life, a grand philosophy. After all, they often acted as though they did. When they said things like, "When you're my age, you'll understand better," that was the impression I got.

And I wanted every grown-up to *stand* for something, as surely as Santa Claus stood for Christmas and the Grim Reaper stood for death. That young radical, with the sardonic grin and the cocked eyebrow—I wanted him to be the personification of everything that was irreverent, cynical and subversive. And that motherly teacher with the soft eyes—I wanted her to be the very embodiment of kindness, responsibility and maturity. If I heard the young radical express a commonplace opinion, or if I heard the motherly teacher make a crude joke, I was extremely put out.

Of course, as I grew older, I began to realize—as every child realizes, sooner or later—that grown-ups weren't really like this at all. Just like kids, they said things they didn't mean. They went through phases and had moods. They claimed to know things that they didn't really know. Worst of all, they were inconsistent. They were not the embodiment or personification of anything—just a bundle of contradictions.

I didn't realize then that there were exceptions to this rule—that there were some grown-ups who really were completely consistent. Fanatics were consistent. Obsessives were consistent. People who were completely dedicated to some single pursuit, whether it was poetry or mathematics or football, were consistent. Then again, such people tended to be consistent at the expense of a sense of humor, or a sense of perspective, or even sanity. And then there were the saints—the saints were consistent. But I didn't know anything about the saints yet.

So, since my longing for specialness and atmosphere and consistency were not satisfied by everyday life, where did I go looking for them? Well, in keeping with my love of Halloween, one of the places I went was the horror genre. In fact, I can't remember a time I didn't love the horror genre—horror movies, ghost stories, and all things spooky. I often hesitate to tell people that I am a horror fan, because it conjures up the wrong images. People have visions of chainsaws and gore and blood. That wasn't really the sort of horror I loved. It was spooky horror I loved, and the whole atmosphere that went with it—crumbling castles, the howl of a wolf in the night, branches tapping at a window, a full moon, a pale face glimpsed in the corner of the mirror...

When I watched a horror movie—as I often did with my two

brothers, sitting on the couch with a blanket draped over our knees to hide under at the scariest parts — I was lost in a world that was *saturated* with an atmosphere all its own, a world where everything was transformed. In a horror movie, things that are entirely prosaic in ordinary life — a footstep, a shadow, a breeze — take on a whole new, menacing, thrilling aspect. The horror genre wasn't the only place I sought refuge from the *thinness* of ordinary life. I also immersed myself in soccer, science fiction, poetry, movies — seeking in every one of them an intensity, a unity, a vividness of atmosphere that ordinary life lacked.

All this time I had been more or less an atheist. I grew up in a Catholic family, and I went to Catholic school, but being a born skeptic I never took any of it very seriously. The older I grew, however, the more the famous words of St. Augustine described my plight: "Lord, you have made us for Yourself, and our hearts are restless till they rest in You." In my early thirties, I began to understand that my deepest hunger was for the sacred — for God. It took months and months of reading and investigation before I was convinced that God really existed, and that the way to find him was through the Catholic Church. So I began to pray the Rosary, and to read the Bible, and to go to Mass. The last especially was a revelation to me. I had been brought to Mass by my mother as a child, and I had hated it. But now, with my increasing hunger for God and the sacred, I lapped it up. In fact, I went as often as I could.

That's how, one Halloween, I found myself going to All Saints' Day Vigil Mass for the first time — a Vigil Mass (of course) being the Mass which is held on the evening before a holy day. That afternoon, I had decided to watch a marathon of horror movies, to get into the Halloween atmosphere. I can remember that the movie entitled *Halloween*, the classic low-budget slasher that spawned a million imitators, was one of the three, but I don't remember the others. Afterwards, I made my way to my local church. The neighborhood was full of trick-or-treaters. Fireworks exploded around me every few moments. I was in a very Halloweeny mood.

The priest was robed in red vestments for the feast day (though white would have been more correct). The congregation was smaller than usual. The church, which I usually attended in morning light, seemed like a different place when it was lit entirely by artificial light. All of this—as well as the contrast with the revelry outside—made this Mass seem especially solemn and supernatural.

And then there were the readings, which are some of the most powerful readings of the entire liturgical year. It seems a little irreverent to say so, but the readings for All Saints' Day almost make this Mass seem like the climax of the Church's calendar—even though that distinction properly belongs to Easter.

The Gospel reading is the passage we call the Beatitudes ("Blessed are the poor in spirit…blessed are they who mourn…blessed are the meek…"), which is the heart of the Sermon on the Mount. The Sermon on the Mount itself might be termed the heart of Jesus's teaching. But it wasn't the Gospel reading which captivated me the most, at that Mass. It was the reading from the Book of Revelation, the reading that describes the triumph of all God's saints at the end of time:

> After this I had a vision of a great multitude,
> which no one could count,
> from every nation, race, people, and tongue.
> They stood before the throne and before the Lamb,
> wearing white robes and holding palm branches in their
> hands.
> They cried out in a loud voice:
> "Salvation comes from our God, who is seated on the throne,
> and from the Lamb." (Revelation 7:9–10)

What could be more *epic* than the scenario described in this passage? This was a vision of the end of every story, the climax of human history—of my own life and everybody's life. This was how it was all going to end. This was the story that included every other story.

And the figures in that "great multitude which no one could count, from every nation, race, people and country"—they would be the saints, the ones whose lives had been a success in the only way that ultimately mattered. They would be those who could say, like St. Paul,

"I have fought the good fight, I have finished the race, I have kept the faith" (2 Timothy 4:7).

The thought that kept running through my head was: so this is what Halloween had been about all along, without my realizing it! Halloween was *The Eve of All Hallows*! Obvious as it sounds, it was a revelation to me.

Vampires, banshees, werewolves, zombies—none of the staples of horror movies were real. But the saints were real. The presence of Our Blessed Lord in the Eucharist was real. Heaven was real. The otherworldliness that had beckoned to me from the horror genre was only a fiction—but the true thing was here, in the Holy Sacrament of the Mass. It was what had been drawing me all along. In the real supernatural world, there was certainly horror—sin, and demons, and the danger of Hell. But there was also wonder, and awe—wonder and awe beyond anything I had glimpsed in any movie, or story, or poem.

The lives of the saints (which I had started to read about, since I had discovered faith) were the ultimate example of all the things I had been craving—specialness, and purity, and vividness. In the words of St. Josemaría Escrivá, founder of Opus Dei, the saints had "transformed the prose of life into poetry." The saints were human beings who had been transformed by Jesus Christ, who had been transformed *into* *images* of Christ. Their lives were completely dedicated to one goal—to live out the gospel. The whiteness of their robes, in the passage from the Book of Revelation, symbolized purity—the kind of purity, the kind of consistency that I looked for in grown-ups when I was a child. Just as Santa Claus was the embodiment of Christmas, and just as the Grim Reaper was the embodiment of death, the saints were the embodiment of the Gospel—living images of Jesus Christ.

And just as All Saints' Day had always lain behind Halloween, without my even realizing it, the idea of sanctity lay unsuspected behind all the worldly images of success and glory and adventure that my society offered me. The superstar, the millionaire, the artist, the rebel—these were all faint images of true success, true wealth, true courage. Underneath all the dramas of life lay the ultimate drama of the quest for holiness.

I have been drawing inspiration from the lives and words of the saints for years now, and this book is my attempt to share some of that inspiration.

As I have said, it is a very personal book. It is by no means an academic treatise, a comprehensive survey, or a reference book. It is, rather, the sort of book about the saints that I have long been looking for myself.

There are many excellent reference books dedicated to the saints, full of dates and details and facts. I must admit that I find them rather dry reading. In reading about the saints, I look instead for human interest — stories, anecdotes, glimpses into their souls. *Inspiration from the Saints* looks at its subject through a series of themes — themes such as childhood, humility, marriage, the Eucharist, and prayer. My focus is more upon modern saints than ancient or medieval saints — simply because I find it easier to relate to them, and because I think today's Catholics may also find it easier to relate to them. However, I do look at some ancient and medieval saints.

Although I have tried to write for a general audience, the book is inevitably written from a particular perspective — that of an Irishman born in the late twentieth century. Growing up in the nineteen-eighties and nineteen-nineties, I just barely caught the sunset years of "Catholic Ireland" — a time when most people in Ireland went to Mass, when bishops and priests were treated with great respect by the media, and when open attacks on Catholicism were very rare. The situation is now completely transformed — the Irish media, Irish politicians, and Irish entertainment figures routinely castigate the Catholic Church. Ireland became the first country to introduce same-sex "marriage" by popular referendum in 2015, and there are powerful campaigns to drive the Church out of education and to remove Ireland's constitutional ban on abortion. Despite this, however, Catholicism remains an everyday presence in Ireland — almost eighty percent of Irish people describe themselves as Catholic, Catholic chapels are to be found in hospitals, airports, and shopping centers, and a huge number of streets, schools, and even private houses are named after Catholic saints.

I am using the term "saints" quite strictly—I will concern myself in this book only with people whom the Catholic Church has officially canonized or beatified.

As many of my readers will know, *canonization* is the act by which the Catholic Church declares a deceased person a saint. *Beatification* is the act by which the Church confers the title "Blessed" on somebody—which is the second-to-last stage in becoming a saint. In modern times, both of these processes are painstaking and can take decades. Let me explain them a little further. When a person is beatified, the Church has confirmed that person is in Heaven. When a person is canonized, the Church is telling Catholics all over the world that this is a person they may venerate, and take as a model of holiness. A beatified person is given the title "Blessed"—Blessed John Henry Newman, for instance. A canonized person is given the title "Saint" (St. for short)—St. John Paul II, for instance. The word "beatus" is sometimes used for a beatified person. For simplicity's sake, I will refer to people who have reached either of these stages as "saints."

"'Servant of God" and "Venerable" are earlier stages on the road to possible canonization. "Servant of God" simply means that the Church is investigating that person's cause for sainthood. (This is the case with my favorite author of all time, G.K. Chesterton.) "Venerable" means that the Church has investigated a person's life and found that he or she lived a life of heroic virtue. Archbishop Fulton J. Sheen, the famous Catholic televangelist of the twentieth century, has attained the title of "Venerable." I have often been disappointed by books that profess to be about the saints, but which include many figures who have not even been beatified yet. For instance, I don't doubt that my beloved G.K. Chesterton is a bona fide saint. I am not, however, going to preempt the Church's decision on that score.

This book doesn't focus very much upon miracles or supernatural visions, except as far as they relate to the themes I have chosen. Such wonders are the extraordinary gifts of God, which most Christians will never experience. However, we can and should seek to emulate the saints in the way they lived their lives, and this is what I concentrate on.

While I expect that most people who read this book will be practicing Catholics, my goal is to make it accessible to non-Catholics, non-Christians and those who may be feeling their way to faith. To cater to these readers, I will explain some basic Catholic concepts as I go along—I hope that experienced Catholic readers will not become impatient with me for this. Those who are steeped in their faith can sometimes forget just how secularized society has become, and that even intelligent, well-read people often now have very little knowledge of Catholicism.

I started this introduction with a memory of a Halloween long ago, one in which I became enthralled with the idea of one night that was dedicated to a particular atmosphere, a particular idea. I found myself craving times and places that were dedicated, that were *special*, in a similar way. And I even wanted people to be similarly dedicated, similarly consecrated to a particular ideal or philosophy. This is what I found in the saints, who are completely dedicated to Jesus Christ.

The name "Christ" actually means "the anointed one." The anointing to which it refers is the holy anointing oil with which the priests and kings of Israel were made holy—the word holy meaning "set apart." Christ was utterly dedicated to his mission—"*My food is to do the will of Him who sent me* and to accomplish His work" (John 4:34). Similarly, the saints were utterly dedicated to following Christ. "For me to live is Christ," St. Paul writes in the New Testament (Philippians 1:21).

The lives of the saints are *all about Christ*. How they lived that out is the subject of this book, one possible book out of the endless number that could be written: "Jesus did many other things as well. If every one of them were written down, I suppose that even the whole world would not have room for the books" (John 21:25). I hope these stories and quotations inspire you, as they have inspired me.

Childhood

*The visionaries of Fatima * St. Aloysius Gonzaga*
*Blessed Anne Catherine Emmerich * St. John Berchmans*
*St. Miguel Pro * St. Elizabeth of the Trinity*

THE VERY EXISTENCE OF CHILDHOOD IS ONE OF the facts (one of the many, many facts) which hint at the existence of a God. Obviously, the human race had to have some way of reproducing itself, or the species would have disappeared long ago. But one can't help seeing the artistry of Providence behind the particular way that it was done.

Childhood is far more than just the period of immaturity that humans go through on their way to adulthood. Imagine if there was some kind of injection that would speed up the process, and that would send us from being a newborn baby to being a fully-grown human in some radically shortened period — a day, or a week, or a month. Let's further suppose that this had no baneful side-effects, and that the adult who thus mushroomed into maturity would be psychologically and emotionally healthy. It still sounds like a nightmare, doesn't it?

Childhood is so much more than a developmental stage. As well as undeveloped bodies and minds, children have assets of their own — wonder, and innocence, and a power of imagination that is the flip side of credulity.

Yes, children hate hearing the assertion that "these are the best years of your life." Who wouldn't? Indeed, it isn't always true — some people have terrible childhoods. But it's certainly true that the joys and pains of childhood are, in many ways, more vivid than anything that comes after. The Halloween party I described earlier is an example of how experiences from childhood — often very simple experiences — can influence our whole outlook and careers as adults.

Of course, it is all too easy to be sentimental about childhood. *Lord of the Flies*, William Golding's classic novel about a group of boys stranded on an island without adults, is a very convincing depiction of the savagery that might easily break out in such a situation. We can probably all remember acts of cruelty and spite in our childhoods which shock us when we look back on them as adults. School playgrounds, in particular, can be ruthless places. Those who criticize the Christian doctrine of original sin (very often with words such as "Are you *really* saying that a little baby is born with sin?") often fail to take this into account. Indeed, Sir John Betjeman's poem "Original Sin on the Sussex Coast," which describes an episode of childhood bullying, explicitly insists on the presence of evil in childhood — "the devil walks" in such incidents, Betjeman writes.

And yet Jesus himself told us that we should imitate children: "Unless you be converted and become like little children, you shall not enter the kingdom of Heaven" (Matthew 18:3). In the next verse we are told that it is the *humility* of children which we are to emulate. Children are well aware of their own littleness. Their complete trust in their parents is the sort of radical trust we should all show in God.

There are many child saints, most of whom were martyrs. Two exceptional cases — child saints who were *not* martyrs, that is — are Jacinta and Francisco Marto, two of the three visionaries to whom Our Blessed Lady revealed herself at Fatima, Portugal, in 1917. A year later, Jacinta and Francisco died in the great flu epidemic that swept through the world after World War One. The cause for their sainthood was ground-breaking, as the Vatican had recently ruled that such causes should not be investigated. Children, it had been decided, were too young to understand the concept of heroic virtue, never mind pursue it. A campaign which was supported by hundreds of bishops led Pope John Paul II to revoke this ruling, and in 2000 the same Pope beatified Juanita and Francisco. In 2017, they were declared saints by Pope Francis.

The facts of Fatima are well known. Three shepherd children (Jacinta, Francisco, and Lucia) experienced six apparitions of the Blessed Virgin, during which they were told to pray the Rosary every day and to perform penances. They were also shown a terrifying vision of Hell, and promised a miracle "so that all will believe." The miracle, which duly occurred on October 13, 1917, was witnessed by tens of thousands of onlookers. The sun was seen to dance in the sky, not only by those who had gathered on the spot where the children had been having their visions of Our Lady, but many miles away. It is undoubtedly the most spectacular miracle of modern times.

The holy lives of the three children of Fatima testify that the miraculous apparitions they witnessed were truly of God. Before the apparitions, they had been ordinary, if pious, children. (They hurried through the rosary as quickly as possible, simply saying "Hail Mary" for each bead, so they would have more time to play!)

After the apparitions, they dedicated their lives to prayer and penance — Lucia until the impressive age of ninety-seven, Jacinta and Francisco until their deaths at the ages of nine and ten. Indeed, Sister Lucia, when writing about the children many years later, remarked: "Jacinta took this matter of making sacrifices for the conversion of sinners so much to heart, that she never let a single opportunity escape her."[1] Even on her deathbed, suffering from thirst, she refused to drink, as she wanted to offer penance right to her last moments. (This desire to share Christ's thirst on the Cross, in the last moments of life, is quite common amongst the saints.)

This anecdote, taken from *Fatima in Lucia's Own Words*, shows what a dedication to penance and charity the children had developed:

> There were two families in Moita whose children used to go round begging from door to door. We met them one day, as we were going along with our sheep. As soon as she saw them, Jacinta said to us:
>
> "Let's give our lunch to those poor children, for the conversion of sinners."
>
> And she ran to take it to them. That afternoon, she told me she was hungry. There were holm-oaks and oak trees nearby.

1 St. Lucia de Jesus dos Santos, *Fatima in Lucia's Own Words: Sister Lucia's Memories* (Fatima, Secretariado Dos Pastorinhos), www.pastorinhos.com/_wp/wp-content/uploads/MemoriasI_en.pdf, accessed 10 December, 2016.

The acorns were still quite green. However, I told her we could eat them.

Francisco climbed up a holm-oak to fill his pockets, but Jacinta remembered that we could eat the ones on the oak trees instead, and thus make a sacrifice by eating the bitter kind. So it was there, that afternoon, that we enjoyed this delicious repast! Jacinta made this one of her usual sacrifices, and often picked the acorns off the oaks or the olives off the trees. One day I said to her:

"Jacinta, don't eat that; it's too bitter!"

"But it's because it's bitter that I'm eating it, for the conversion of sinners."[2]

It's true that these children had gone through an experience the like of which is vouchsafed only to a tiny minority of the human race. But they were still children, and they still lived lives of heroic virtue. The desire for holiness was something urgent and immediate to them, not a vague aspiration. Seeing this in the lives of these children impresses on the rest of us, not only the *reality* of holiness, but the fact that *holiness is achievable* — even little children like these could attain it. Can adults really claim that it is beyond their reach?

The story of the lives of the Fatima children also emphasizes the fact that they understood ideas such as sin, holiness and penance, and that these are not complicated ideas. True, vast volumes of moral theology have been written on these matters, and these are of much value — the truths of the Christian faith are no less deep, no less amenable to analysis, than the truths of science and history and other fields of human knowledge.

But there is a temptation to take an excessively sophisticated approach to Christianity, one which all too often means that our faith becomes whatever we want it to be — people who suffer from this tend to dismiss unquestioning piety as "literal-minded" and "simplistic." Faith becomes a matter of seminars, retreats, lectures, insights, erudition. With this approach, we teeter towards *gnosticism*, the age-old

2 Ibid.

heresy which takes innumerable forms, but which always promises enlightenment through some kind of advanced knowledge.

Against this, how refreshing is the story of these shepherd children giving up their lunches and making innumerable other sacrifices, prostrating themselves in prayer so that their heads touched the ground (as an angel had shown them to), and—in the case of Jacinta and Francisco—meeting their early deaths with such bravery! Please notice, as well, St. Jacinta's insistence on penance *for the conversion of sinners.* There was an evangelistic and soul-saving dimension to the children's sacrifices. They wanted not only to seek God, but to lead others to God—the Christian God.

The Fatima visionaries: St. Jacinta, Lucia, and St. Francisco

The idea has grown up in our modern society that sainthood is simply a matter of moral excellence, moral perfection. But Christian sainthood (and Christian life in general) *must be concerned with the salvation of souls and the spread of the Gospel* if it is to be Christian at all. This is a theme we will meet again and again in the lives of the saints. Their charity was not simple philanthropy, but always had a supernatural aspect to it.

Even looking at the pictures of the three Fatima visionaries strikes one with a certainty of their holiness and their authenticity. Their faces are filled with the simplicity and directness of childhood, and also with that elusive characteristic called sanctity.

But it isn't only child-saints who have lived holy childhoods. In fact, it is surprisingly common for saints to have been outstandingly pious from an early age. Take the example of St. Aloysius Gonzaga. The son of the Marquis of Castiglione in Italy, he became a Jesuit, and died in 1591 at the age of twenty-three, after heroically caring for the victims of an epidemic. Legend has it that St. Aloysius's first words were "Jesus" and "Mary." (This is a tradition we encounter in the lives of many saints, but that is not to say that it is not true.) He took a private vow of perpetual virginity at the age of nine, having been so moved by a particular passage in a book about the Virgin Mary that he felt the urge to do some special thing to please her. At ten he vowed never to offend God by sinning — a vow that St. Robert Bellarmine (a contemporary of St. Gonzaga's and a future Doctor of the Church), who heard Aloysius's confessions, judged him to have kept. So comparatively sinless was Aloysius that two minor trespasses as a child — letting off a cannon without permission, and repeating some bad language picked up from soldiers without even understanding it — weighed on him for the rest of his days. He would mention these as examples of his bad behavior all through his life, to convince others that he was not as saintly as he seemed.

Even as a child, Aloysius fasted three days a week on bread and water, made shrines and altars as a hobby, and would hide himself in corners of the house so that he could pray uninterrupted. And he had such a devotion to his vow of chastity that he avoided so much as looking at women — indeed, he even avoided being alone with his own mother. (Given that she was the initial source of piety in his life — she wished him to be a priest, but his soldier father opposed it — one might wonder if she felt any indignation at his taking his piety this far!) Servants would peep through the chinks in St. Aloysius's door to see him lying before his crucifix, for hours at a time, praying with his arms outstretched. He was also heard saying a Hail Mary at every step, when walking upstairs or downstairs. And he delighted in reading about the lives of the saints — this, too, is something we encounter again and again in the stories of saints.

The childhood of St. Aloysius may seem priggish, cold, and excessive in its piety to us. But let us remember the words of Oscar Wilde: "Nothing succeeds like excess." The saints are remarkable for their *heroic* virtue, and the stories we remember and tell about them are usually about extraordinary feats.

Here is an example from modern, secular life which might help us to put the extravagances of St. Aloysius (and other saints) in perspective. F. Scott Fitzgerald, author of *The Great Gatsby*, once had dinner with the Irish novelist James Joyce. At this time, Fitzgerald was a young man, and Joyce was internationally celebrated. The younger writer was so star-struck that he offered to jump out the window as an expression of his admiration. Joyce very sensibly forbade this, but the anecdote seems a good illustration of how extravagantly people behave under the influence of some strong devotion. The devotion that the saints felt to our Lord Jesus Christ manifested itself in much extravagant behavior, even (in many cases) in childhood. There's really nothing very strange about this. It is a very human response.

Let us remember how Jesus reacted when a woman who had lived a sinful life (traditionally identified as St. Mary Magdalen) poured ointment over him and kissed his feet, during his visit to the house of Simon the leper. Far from chastising her, he defended her when she was chastised by others. In the same way, he defended those who threw palms in front of him and shouted as he entered Jerusalem. Our Lord obviously does not disapprove of extravagance in the right places, and for the right motives.

I could fill this entire book with instances of extravagant piety in the childhoods of the saints. Though there are many saints who were decided sinners in their early days, there are also a great number of saints who seem to have been saintly from their cradles. Here is a simple example, from the life of Blessed Anne Catherine Emmerich, a German mystic who died in 1824, and whose visions of the life of Christ had an influence on the Mel Gibson film *The Passion of the Christ*, which was such a massive success in 2004:

Anne Catherine Emmerich, when trying to practice her reading by the light of burning chips of wood, would choose chips from new planks, with which her father was mending a neighbor's bench. When her father suggested old chips would make better firewood, she declined to use them because they were their neighbor's property.[3]

There is a charming story from the life of St. Frances Xavier Cabrini, foundress of the Missionary Sisters of the Sacred Heart. As a young child in Italy, she would make paper boats and fill them with violets, imagining the violets were missionaries going abroad to win converts. At one point, however, she fell into the lake, thus developing a long-standing fear of deep water — a fear which she overcame when she brought her Order to serve the spiritual needs of Italian immigrants in America. Another story from her childhood has her family looking for her after an earthquake had hit their home. They found her lost in prayer, completely oblivious to what had happened.

A saint who was greatly influenced by St. Aloysius Gonzaga, and in fact took him as his model, was the Belgian St. John Berchmans. St. Berchmans was a Jesuit seminarian — that is, a young man who was training to be a priest in the Jesuit order — who died at the age of twenty-two, never living to make his final vows. He died in Rome while participating in a philosophical debate organized by the Dominicans. His sanctity was recognized immediately.

St. Berchmans was a saint even in childhood, as one biographer explains:

> From his first years, the child foreshadowed the exceptional gifts which were to make him the model of a sanctity which is lovable and gracious. He was never any trouble to anyone. He bore, without crying, the little trials of his tender age; and attacks of sicknesses to which children are subject and which render the best of them irritable and hard to manage, never drew from him

---

3 Edith Renouf, *Life of Catherine Emmerich* (1950), 10.

any sign of complaint. No oppositions ever elicited from him
any sign of complaint. No opposition from him ever elicited any
gesture of impatience. Sometimes when he came back home, it
happened that he found the doors locked. The child then called
to mind a house in which he was at home with his Father. He
went into the church and recited his rosary.

St. John Berchmans

It was a recompense to John's religious parents to see the spontaneous blossoming of the germs of piety which they had made it their study to plant in the soul of the child. Every morning he went to the parish church to assist at the Holy Sacrifice, and when, at the age of seven, he began to go to school, of his own accord he arose earlier so as not to go to class without having served two or three Masses.[4]

If all this gives the impression that all saints were perfect children, perhaps the reader will find some relief in stories that prove this is not so. St. Miguel Pro was a Jesuit who was martyred in 1927, during a persecution of the Catholic Church by an anti-Catholic Mexican government. His life is full of stories of dashing heroism—he was something of a priestly James Bond, constantly on the run from the authorities and often slipping right through their fingers. But he wasn't above a little bit of naughtiness as a child:

> Miguel's thoughts dwelt often on tortillas—maize cakes capable of a wonderful diversity; he was in fact a fairly greedy little boy. Once all funds for the purchase of *dulce*, of sweets, had run out. There was a compliant [obliging] sweet merchant, but even he hesitated: "Have no fear," said Miguel, his black eyes bravely encountering those of the doubtful sweet vendor. "Put it down to my mother." The performance was repeated till the sum totaled up was respectable and the merchant sent in his bill…the Senora paid it, but so did her little boy, but with a difference. Miguel remembered the payment for some time in the body but always in the mind.[5]

The future saint also threw a tantrum when his beloved sisters decided to enter religious life:

4 Hippolyte Delehaye, *St. John Berchmans* (New York, Benziger Brothers, 1921), 18–19.
5 Mrs. George Norman, *God's Jester: The Story of the Life and Martyrdom of Fr. Michael Pro* (New York, Benziger Brothers, 1930), 6–7.

Two of his sisters were going to enter convents, to be nuns. Miguel was astounded; no, he was outraged. His sisters, part of his family, to be torn away; the happy, good, life round the flowering patios, the peaceful, gay round of good works and family reunions, of quite legitimate amusements, the family prayers, the Sunday Masses with the two beloved charming girls in their high combs and mantillas, the walks by the fountain, the music-making, all this to end, at any rate for them, his dark-eyed sisters....

He went into the brushwoods and stayed there.... He was there for days, and then someone, his mother—as she would have done—found him. She got him to go home; alarmed no doubt at this outburst, this unbridled impetuosity, this rebellion, she talked to him, with her gentleness, her firmness. She wanted him—Miguel!—to go to make a retreat, that is to retire for a few days' reflection and prayer into some religious house. It is a common enough procedure amongst Catholics, but it was the last thing Miguel wanted to do. In the end he went.[6]

Miguel went reluctantly to the retreat, but it set him on the road to sainthood and martyrdom. We will encounter him again later.

A recently canonized saint, St. Elizabeth of the Trinity, is an even more striking example of a holy person who was far from holy in childhood. This French mystic, who died as a Carmelite nun in 1906, had such a stubborn streak as a young girl, and was prone to such rages, that her mother told her "you will either be a terror, or a saint." After her first confession she learned to control her temper, and, though she yearned to be a Carmelite nun from an early age, she patiently obeyed her mother's request that she wait until the age of twenty-one. She died only five years later, of Addison's disease (a disorder of the adrenal glands). Although she performed no remarkable feats in her short life, her personal holiness and her writings on mental prayer led Pope Francis to declare her a saint in October 2016.

6 Ibid., 10–11.

I include these stories because, in their own way, they are as inspiring as the stories of St. Aloysius Gonzaga and the children of Fatima. The picture of little children completely dedicated to the worship of God shows us that such dedication is possible, even for children. As well, this image shows us that God is something that can satisfy our entire heart and soul, and do not most human beings yearn for such satisfaction? If we are tempted to think that we can never reach such heights — if we are tempted to think that our petty and selfish and wayward impulses are too strong, and too many — the stories of saints who have been far from saintly in childhood remind us that this is not so.

Sinners

St. Paul of Tarsus ✳ *St. Augustine of Hippo*
St. Philip Howard ✳ *St. Bernard of Corleone*
Blessed Bartolo Longo ✳ *Blessed Charles de Foucauld*

NAUGHTY CHILDREN ARE ONE THING, BUT WHAT about serious wrongdoing in adulthood? It's reassuring to know that several people who fell deep into grave sin at some point in their lives eventually made the Church's list of saints. "The greater the sinner, the greater the saint" is a well-known proverb on this topic; it seems to have originated in the eighteenth century with the Methodist preacher George Whitefield. So in itself, it doesn't seem to be a sentiment that has any backing in the Catholic tradition.

However, the twentieth century Polish mystic St. Faustina—who was granted many private revelations—was told by Our Blessed Lord that "the greater the sinner, the greater the claim he has to my Mercy." Catholics are not required to believe in private revelations (that is, revelations outside the public revelation of Scripture). However, given that Faustina is a saint, and that the Church celebrates Divine Mercy Sunday every year as a result of her private revelations, the revelations vouchsafed to her should surely carry considerable weight. Besides, the Bible itself says something very similar: "There will be more rejoicing in heaven over one sinner who repents than over ninety-nine righteous persons who do not need to repent" (Luke 15:7).

Similarly, there is the New Testament story already mentioned, of the woman who poured perfume over Jesus's feet in the house of Simon the leper, and who wet them with her tears and wiped them with her hair. In response to Simon's (unspoken) thought that the woman was a notorious sinner, Jesus explains that those who have experienced greater forgiveness show greater love, as the woman's lavish demonstration of love towards him proves. Traditionally, this woman was identified with St. Mary Magdalene, to whom the first post-Resurrection appearance of Jesus mentioned in the gospels was made. Today there seems to be no consensus on this matter.

St. Paul of Tarsus, whose letters to various early Christian churches form a large part of the New Testament, is another Biblical example of a notorious sinner turned saint. St. Paul was originally a Pharisee called Saul who energetically persecuted the early Christians. Indeed, we read of him guarding the cloaks of those who stoned St. Stephen, the first martyr, and he tells us himself in one of his letters that he approved of the stoning.

Of course, Saul had his famous vision of Our Lord on the road to Damascus, and from that moment went from being the most ardent persecutor of Christianity to being one of its most zealous disciples. As he wrote himself: "For I am the least of the apostles and do not even deserve to be called an apostle, because I persecuted the church of God" (1 Corinthians 15:9).

St. Augustine of Hippo, the greatest of the Fathers of the Church, is another famous sinner turned saint. He lived with a mistress for fifteen years, even having a son by her, before converting to Christianity and committing himself to a life of celibacy.

A saint who is less well known, but whose life makes a fascinating story, is St. Philip Howard of England (1557–1595). England at this time was a very dangerous place to be a Catholic, since the English Reformation had taken place and Catholicism was treated as treason. Although he was eventually to give his life for his faith — condemned to death, he was not actually executed, but died in prison — St. Philip had a far from holy life in his early days. He was an ambitious courtier, at a time when success at court meant flattering and pleasing the immensely vain Queen Elizabeth. He spent enormous sums in order to live the expensive life of a courtier, putting on entertainments for the Queen, as well as giving her gifts which include (to quote contemporary reports): "a girdle of tawny velvet embroidered with seed pearls, the buckle and pendant [made] of gold; a pair of bracelets of gold containing eight pieces in every of them an amethyst, and eight other pieces, and in every of them a pearl;

a carcanet (necklace) of gold containing seven pieces of gold, six true loves of small sparks of diamonds, and many pearls of sundry bigness and small sparks of rubies."[1] In fact, he put himself into such debt, trying to gain the Queen's favor, that he had to sell some of his land — and not only his own land, but that belonging to his wife. What makes this all the more remarkable is that his father had been executed by the same Queen for involvement in a plot against her.

St. Philip Howard

While Philip was living it up at court, he was also ignoring his wife, to whom he had been married since they were both fourteen. Eventually she went to live with his grandfather, the Earl of Arundel. Though he showed charity to the poor, his life was fundamentally one of self-seeking and frivolity.

1 Cecil Kerr, *The Life of the Ven. Philp Howard, Earl of Arundel and Surrey* (London: Longmans, Green and Co. Ltd., 1926), 30.

It was listening to a debate between a Catholic and two Protestants that changed St. Philip's life. The Catholic was another saint, St. Edmund Campion, who would eventually be martyred. He was a brilliant Jesuit who, at the time of the debates, was a prisoner and had already been tortured several times. Despite these conditions, he performed very well against his Protestant opponents. Philip Howard was in the audience for one of these debates, and was deeply impressed. Slowly, he began to be drawn to the Catholic faith, eventually being received into the Church. His sister and wife had already converted.

Catholicism was illegal in England at this time, and Philip — who had by this time inherited the title of Earl of Arundel (a title that had been thrown into question his by father's execution) — was such a prominent person that he found it very difficult to hide his religious beliefs. His refusal to condemn his wife's religion, and his reluctance to participate in non-Catholic religious services, threw suspicion on him. He was just about to leave England, so that he could practice his religion abroad, when he was arrested and imprisoned in the infamous Tower of London. He would stay there for the remaining ten years of his life, though he was promised freedom if he renounced his faith. On the wall of his cell, he wrote a Latin inscription which translates: "The more afflictions we endure for Christ in this world, the more glory we shall obtain with Christ in the next."

The story of St. Philip Howard is especially inspiring because his transformation is so unexpected. Before his conversion, he was simply another courtier hanging around the court of Queen Elizabeth I, hoping to win the all-important favor of the Queen. His neglect of his wife is especially mean-spirited and unattractive — not even the kind of hot-blooded sin which might hint at great energies and passions within, the sort of personality of which saints are made. Furthermore, St. Philip would have been well aware that converting to Catholicism might have very bad consequences for him, in the England of the time. Everything in his life seemed to make the step he took most unlikely. His story seems that of a man who has become intellectually convinced that the Catholic faith is the truth, and chosen his path accordingly.

In more recent times, we have a saint who seriously wounded a man in a duel. Filippo Latini was a Sicilian of the seventeenth century who was famous for his skill with a sword, and was always quick to get into a fight. Despite this, he was quite pious, even begging for food on behalf of the poor. Nevertheless, Filippo's enthusiasm for sword fighting led him to accept a challenge from one Vito Canino. Filippo inflicted a near-fatal wound on Canino, cutting off his arm, and hurried to a Capuchin Franciscan friary out of fear of revenge. (An appropriate haven, as it happened, as he already had quite a devotion to St. Francis.)

Although he was forgiven by the man he had attacked, the incident made Filippo take stock of his life, and he eventually joined the Capuchins as a lay brother (that is, a friar who is not ordained as a priest). He took the religious name Bernard, becoming known as Bernard of Corleone. His life after that was one of exemplary penance and sanctity — he slept on a plank bed, whipped himself regularly (a surprisingly common practice in the lives of the saints, used to gain control over the body and to repent for sins — we will discuss austerities and penance in another chapter), and was known for his gentleness and charity. He was illiterate, but when it was suggested to him that he should learn how to read and write, he said that the only thing he needed to study were the wounds of Christ. It was not until 2001 that he was made a saint, by John Paul II — he had been beatified more than two hundred years before, in 1768!

Even more spectacular than this is the case of Bartolo Longo, the former Satanist who was beatified. Really!

Bartolo, born in Southern Italy in 1841, was a gifted and charismatic young man from a devout Catholic family, in which the rosary was said every night. However, when he went to law school, he had the same experience as so many other students from a Christian background — he encountered professors who were strongly hostile to the Catholic faith, and who ridiculed it.

Not only did this turn him against his childhood religion, but he was even drawn to a fascination with the occult and witchcraft, which were fashionable at the time. He attended séances (a practice which is extremely dangerous for the soul, and strictly forbidden to Catholics), and eventually sank to the depths of being ordained a priest in a Satanic cult. At this time, he not only rejected Christianity himself, but even tried to push others away from it—something that would weigh very heavily upon him in the future.

Blessed Bartolo Longo

The occult practices he was following involved rigorous fasting. One particular bout of fasting led him to fall sick, and this was accompanied by a mental breakdown. As misfortunate as this may have seemed at first, it was in fact the beginning of his salvation. The prayers of his mother should also be mentioned, which remind us of the prayers of St. Monica for her son, St. Augustine—a story we will come to presently. (How much good in this world is achieved by mothers' prayers!) At this time, Bartolo head the voice of his deceased father saying to him: "Return to God, return to God."

The return was not to be an instant affair. It required a conversation with a Christian professor, a friend of his mother. The professor was horrified to hear about Bartolo's occult practices. He put him in contact with a Dominican priest, Fr. Alberto Radente, who led him back to the faith of his childhood, heard his confession and gave him absolution. At this time, Bartolo also became a member of the Third Order of St. Dominic — a lay member of the Dominican Order.

In penance for his time as a Satanist, Bartolo Longo began to speak to students in the university from which he had now graduated, mingling with them in cafés and parties, and telling them how he had become embroiled in the occult. He was an effective evangelist, and led many students towards the faith. However, he wished to do still more, in order to redeem his past.

Bartolo was now a practicing lawyer, and one of his clients was a woman in Pompeii (close to the site of Vesuvius) called Countess Marianna Farnararo De Fusco. When he visited Pompeii, he was appalled by the religious ignorance of the people there, along with the popularity of the same spiritualistic practices he had rejected. Remembering a promise made by Our Lady to St. Dominic — "Whoever propagates my rosary will be saved" — Bartolo decided to spread devotion to the holy rosary amongst the religiously lax people of Pompeii. The Countess De Fusco was his partner in this enterprise. In fact, they eventually got married — at the suggestion of the Pope himself! They did this to avoid the gossip that might rise from a single man and a single woman working so closely together. They had both taken private vows of chastity, so they did not have physical relations.

This strange married couple worked together to spread devotion to the rosary. Bartolo held several "rosary festivals," which were not successful at first; the first priest he asked to preach didn't even speak the local dialect. The festivals did, however, eventually take off. Bartolo also restored two churches, using funds donated by the people, and enshrined a picture of Our Lady which — although taken from a junk shop, and lacking any great artistic merit — immediately began to be associated with miracles. Bartolo continued to promote the rosary until his death at the age of eighty-five, and was beatified in 1980 by Pope John Paul II.

I can't end this chapter without mentioning the extraordinary case of Blessed Charles de Foucauld (1858–1916), whose life is like a modern repeat of the story of St. Augustine—both of them men of great intellect and character, both of them particularly attracted to the sins of the flesh before their conversions, both of them drawn to mortification afterwards. Indeed, Blessed Charles went from needing a special army uniform made for him because he was so fat, to leaving the Trappist order because they started to allow butter on parsnips!

Blessed Charles de Foucauld

He was born of a noble family in Strasbourg, of a family with strong military traditions. Through devout in childhood, he stopped practicing in his teens, greatly influenced by the skeptical atmosphere of the time. By this time, he had become an orphan. He went to military school, where he became known for his life of ostentation and pleasure. Once, enjoying a bottle of wine in a hotel, he bought the entire stock at a cost of thousands of francs. He also kept mistresses, one of whom he brought to North Africa when he was posted there. As he himself said of these years in his life: "I was all egotism, vanity, impiety, with every desire for evil—I was, as it were, mad."

However, in North Africa, he was touched by the faith of the Muslims he encountered. He was so interested in the region that he came back disguised as a Jewish rabbi, as most of Morocco was forbidden to Christians. His exploration of the country was pioneering, and he wrote a two-volume work which was lauded by all Paris when he returned to France.

He started going to church, even though he was not yet a believer, and this was his prayer: "God, if you exist, let me know you!" He sought advice from a Catholic priest whose air of happiness had impressed him; he found the priest in his confessional, and asked him to come out to speak to him. The priest insisted Charles should come in, confess, and then receive communion, which Charles did. Faith came back to him at this moment, and as he put it: "As soon as I came to believe there was a God, I understood that I could not do otherwise than live only for Him." (This might be taken as the motto of all the saints.)

Charles went to join a Trappist monastery in Syria. However, he was unsatisfied even with the austerity of this famously austere order—he had, as he said, been living more simply in Morocco during his tour of that country. So he went to live in Nazareth for three years, imitating the life of Jesus in the town where he had grown up. He lived in a shed, ate very simple food, and did odd jobs for a congregation of Poor Clare nuns.

He returned to France to be ordained a priest. Then, in imitation of Jesus's searching after the "lost sheep," he went to the most distant place he could think of, the Sahara desert—or, more accurately, an oasis in the Sahara desert called Beni Abbés, where he had a small chapel built and spent many hours in Eucharistic Adoration. He hoped others might come to form a religious community, but this did not come to pass.

Blessed Charles next moved to Algeria to minister to the Tuareg, a desert people. For ten years he studied their language, even writing a translation of the Gospel in it. Although he hoped to win conversions through the witness of his life, he only converted a single old woman. Nor did he ever live to see the religious order he hoped to found; several orders were inspired by his example, but after his death. The Little Brothers of Jesus, The Little Brothers of the Gospel, and the Little Sisters of Jesus are their names. These go in small groups to live and work amongst ordinary people throughout the world.

Blessed Charles de Foucauld was murdered in 1916, by a group of Algerian militants. They had apparently been hoping to capture and ransom him, but when they were challenged by French soldiers, one of their number panicked and shot him through the head. Thus ended one of the most remarkable of all saints' lives — and proof, along with the other stories in this chapter, that even those who seem furthest from God can mend their ways and achieve sanctity.

Inspirations

St. Augustine of Hippo ✳ *St. Anthony of Egypt*
St. Josemaría Escrivá ✳ *St. John of God*
St. Raphaela Mary of the Sacred Heart
St. Mary of the Incarnation

IN HIS POEM "TO THE MAN AFTER THE HARROW,"
Patrick Kavanagh coined the memorable phrase "the mist where Genesis
begins." That mist—the mist in which *the very beginning of something*
is so often enshrouded—is a fascinating subject for study. In scientific
matters, it is relatively easy—at least in principle—to discover how
something begins. We know that a new human being begins when an
ovum is fertilized, for instance. But in the life of the mind and life of
the soul, beginnings are much more…well, misty.

Take the example of music. There is a fascinating book called *A Hard
Day's Write* which attempts the document the inspiration behind every
Beatles song. The author, Steve Turner, does an excellent job tracking
down possible sources for all the songs of the Fab Four. However, in
many cases, it's really impossible to say *where* the idea for a song came
from. For instance, in the cemetery where John Lennon and Paul
McCartney first met, there is a tombstone for a woman named Eleanor
Rigby—which, of course, is the title of a well-known Beatles song.
McCartney, when this was pointed out to him decades after the song
was released, said that he had never noticed any such tombstone, but
admitted that he may have seen it and remembered it subconsciously.
Sometimes, however, there are moments of sudden inspiration, when a
person is struck by a thought or an idea that changes the whole course
of their lives—sometimes, even the course of history.

These are often called "Eureka!" moments, referring to a story in
which the ancient Greek genius Archimedes, upon working out a

solution to a problem that had dogged him for some time, jumped from his bath and shouted "Eureka!" The lives of the saints are full of what we might call spiritual "Eureka!" moments — moments of inspiration and insight, moments when the grace of God struck the saint with the force of a lightning bolt.

St. Augustine of Hippo

Undoubtedly the most famous "Eureka!" moment in the lives of the saints comes (once again) from the life of St. Augustine (354–430), as recorded in his *Confessions*. Augustine, at the age of thirty-one, was working as a professor of rhetoric in Milan, and had been searching for a philosophy to live by all his life. He had pursued, but ultimately rejected, the religion of Manichaeism when he found it could not give him the answers he sought. At the time of the famous scene recorded in his *Confessions*, St. Augustine was being drawn towards Christianity, but he was held back by "the sins of the flesh." One day, his internal conflict reached such an intensity that he found himself weeping beneath a fig tree in the garden of his lodging. At that moment he heard the voice of a child—he could not tell if it was a boy or a girl—chanting "Take it up and read, take it up and read."

Not being able to see the child, he interpreted this as a sign from God, and opened the copy of the New Testament which he had left nearby. The first words he saw were: "Not in rioting and drunkenness, not in chambering and wantonness, not in strife and envying, but put on the Lord Jesus Christ, and make no provision for the flesh to fulfill the lusts thereof" (Romans 13:13–14). These words inspired him, not only to be baptized, but to embrace a life of celibacy. Eventually, he became a bishop and a Doctor of the Church. There is something enthralling about the story; like the story of Archimedes and the bath, it is a timeless moment that echoes through the ages.

Interestingly, St. Augustine had been reading the life of St. Anthony of Egypt (c. 251–356) at this time. A similar moment of inspiration occurs in the life of St. Anthony, who is often (not quite accurately) considered the father of monasticism. Anthony walked into a church at the moment that this text from Mark's gospel was being read aloud: "If you would be perfect, go sell all you have, give it to the poor and come follow me." St. Anthony decided to do just that, selling his property, living a monastic life, and eventually going to live in the desert.

Perhaps my favorite such story—which also concerns one of my favorite saints—is the story of how St. Josemaría Escrivá (1902–1975), founder of Opus Dei, discovered his vocation. Josemaria was a fairly ordinary boy, from a devout and happy family in the Spanish province of Aragon. When he was a sixteen years old, and intending to become an architecture student, he went out on a snowy morning and saw the marks of a bare foot imprinted in the snow. He realized that these belonged to one of the "Discalced" (i.e., shoeless) Carmelite friars who had recently moved into the area. The young Josemaria was so moved by the sight of this sacrifice for God that he resolved to emulate it: "If others make such sacrifices for God and neighbor, can't I offer something?"

Although he quickly decided he wanted to be a priest, he knew that there was something more that God wanted from him. As he wrote later: "Why did I become a priest? Because I thought it would be easier that way to fulfill something God wanted, which I did not know. For about eight years before my ordination I had intimations of it, but I did not know what it was. And I did not come to know until 1928. That is why I became a priest."[1] Nineteen twenty-eight! A full ten years after he had seen the footprints of the snow. Through all this time, while pursuing his priestly formation, legal studies and a very active ministry as a priest and hospital chaplain, the future saint continued to discern his calling, spending long hours before the Blessed Sacrament and praying: "Lord, let me see! Lord, let it be! What is it you want and I do not know?"

On October 2, 1928, Fr. Josemaria finally saw the path he was to take, as he was going over some notes in his room. Suddenly, he saw what it was God was asking for him; to help ordinary Catholics sanctify their secular work and occupations, so that they could become saints without leaving their stations in life. Opus Dei, the name for the organization which sprang from this vision, simply means "the Work of God." (St. Josemaría insisted on avoiding any name that could be used as an adjective, such as Dominican or Franciscan. At first he hoped to avoid having a name for "the Work" at all.) At that memorable moment, he fell to his knees in grateful prayer to God, while church bells rang out to mark the feast of the Guardian Angels. Opus Dei is now a worldwide association with almost 94,000 members—priests, married people, and lay people who have committed to a life of celibacy. It operates schools, university residences, cultural centers, and other institutions.

1 Salvador Bernal, *Msgr. Josemaría Escrivá de Belaguer: A Profile of the Founder of Opus Dei* (Dublin: Veritas, 1977), 62.

Image of St. Josemaría Escrivá

The hurdles St. Josemaría had to overcome to bring "the Work" into being, however, were formidable. In the first place, the organization had no equivalent in the Catholic Church, and it was not until 1950 that it was given papal approval, by Pope Pius XII. Its exact standing in Church law was not finalized until 1982, several years after St. Josemaría's death. In its early years, the outbreak of the Spanish Civil War meant that it was almost destroyed at birth. Furthermore, many sincere Catholics were suspicious of its new ideas—St. Josemaría called this "the opposition of the good" — and this contributed to the opposition it faced.

Even today, Opus Dei is seen as a sinister organization by many — indeed, the albino assassin in *The Da Vinci Code*, the mega-selling pot-boiler by Dan Brown, was an Opus Dei monk (despite the fact that Opus Dei has no monks). Such conspiracy theories and sensationalism will appear ridiculous to anyone who has met members of Opus Dei. One cannot help but be struck by their cheerfulness, their sincerity, and their dedication to the Catholic faith. Every day thousands of them, all over the world, seek to sanctify themselves through their ordinary work — indeed, to sanctify their ordinary work itself. And all of this sprang from an inspiration given to a young Spanish priest on the Feast of the Guardian Angels, in a little room, in response to a decade's worth of prayers.

Why is St. Josemaría's story so compelling? There are many reasons, but one is that it seems like a very clear case of divine inspiration. Christians have a tendency to see providence at work in all sorts of coincidences and apparent signs. While we can never overstate God's involvement in the world, sometimes these claims may seem a bit of a stretch, and not very convincing to a skeptical listener. However, in St. Josemaría's case, it would seem that only willful blindness could deny that providence was at work; the saint's powerful feeling of being called to some unknown work, the long period of discernment, the sudden revelation, and the amazing fruition — which very closely followed St. Josemaría's initial vision, as we shall see.

Another saint who had a memorable moment of inspiration was St. John of God (1495–1550). His pioneering care for the physically and mentally ill led to the foundation of the Brothers Hospitallers of St. John of God, a religious order that ministers to sick people all over the world.

At the time of his inspiration, Joao Duarte Cidade (as he was born) was living in Grenada, Spain, and working as a bookseller. He'd already had a varied life, having been a homeless orphan, a shepherd, and a soldier. One day, in Grenada, he heard an open-air sermon delivered by another saint, St. John of Avila. The theme of the sermon was Christ's love for us, the price he has paid for our liberation, and our failure to respond adequately to that love and that sacrifice. This is how one of St. John of God's biographers, Jose Marie Javierre, describes the reaction of the future saint, as he returned to the town with the rest of the crowd:

> Among those who took the second pathway was a man who appeared to be completely deranged. He was gesticulating in a bizarre way and shouting out as he beat his chest with his fists. The crowd stood aside to let him pass, some were indifferent to him, others felt sorry for the poor wretch. Some even may have recognized him. It is the bookseller from Elvira Gate! What happened to him? They could hear only his shouts for God's mercy.
>
> He has gone mad! There were plenty of potholes full of water in the Cuesta de Gomerez. Juan threw himself into one of these, putting his head into the muddy water, smearing mud on his face and pulling at his hair. He threw his arms about, telling everyone there that he was a sinner. Then he picked himself up again and began to run down the slope, dodging in and out of the people as he went.[2]

When he reached his bookshop, he began to thrash the place, burning his secular books and giving away his religious books for free. Perhaps it is not surprising that he soon found himself inside a mental hospital. Good, however, was to spring from this apparent madness; the saint's first-hand experience of the cruel "treatment" doled out to mental patients, which included whipping and starving, inspired him to pioneer a more enlightened and caring treatment of the mentally ill after he was released.

St. John begged through the streets on behalf of the poor and sick of Grenada. He advertised this as a golden opportunity for donors to pile up treasure in Heaven. He was not content to wait for the indigent to come to him themselves, but went out seeking those who were too

---

2 Jose Maria Javierre, *John of God: Loco in Granada* (Fineline Print Pty Ltd., 1996), 270.

ashamed to ask for help. He was even known to carry the sick on his own shoulders. As is so often the case in the lives of the saints, his example attracted followers, which became the Order of Hospitallers — named (after his death) the Order of Hospitallers of St. John of God. Today they operate hospitals and other services in over fifty countries. Quite a legacy for one sermon!

St. Raphaela Mary of the Sacred Heart (1850–1925), foundress of the Handmaids of the Sacred Heart order, had a less spectacular "wake-up call" than St. John of God — but, in some ways, a more jolting one. Born Raphaela de Porras, she was the daughter of a wealthy family in Spain, and she had a priest for a tutor. One day, when he saw her admiring herself in the mirror, this tutor asked: "How do you think you will look a quarter hour after your death?" This question had such an impact on her that she described it as her conversion.

Along with her sister, she entered religious life after her mother died. Eventually, she founded her own order, and was elected Superior, but jealousy amongst the other sisters led her to resign from her position. She was forced to perform menial jobs, and a rumor spread that she was mentally subnormal. She bore all this with great patience, and eventually attained a reputation for sanctity. Her own reflections on her usurpation are most moving:

> My life has always been a struggle, but the last two years my sufferings have been so extraordinary that it is only by the omnipotence of God which miraculously upholds me at every moment that I have not been beaten to the ground. What horrible sufferings of all kind, in body, soul and heart! My whole being is in continuous straits, and I am without succor, but with the prospect of this state becoming worse and worse.
>
> Do I think, on this account, that I am abandoned by God? No. But my trust in God is in my soul like a frail thread in danger always of breaking; but all the time I go on strengthening it so that I may not fail.... Do you know what I have achieved? The deepest tranquility and repose, and the desire to suffer even more,

and to bear it all in silence. I am resolved to offer myself to God's holy will in complete forgetfulness of myself.[3]

Ironically, given the question of her priest tutor when she was eyeing herself in the mirror as a girl, St. Raphaela Mary's body remained incorrupt for many years after her death.

So far I have dealt with those moments of inspiration, in the lives of saints, which involve no necessarily supernatural elements. These are the stories which seem easiest to relate to for most of us. However, the lives of the saints swarm with stories of life-transforming visions and apparitions. The experience of the three child visionaries of Fatima, which I have already discussed, is one example.

Another saint who had a life-changing supernatural experience — one that came in the form of a dream — was St. Mary of the Incarnation (1599–1672), a French widow who worked to spread the Ursuline order of religious sisters in Quebec, Canada. The Ursulines worked to educate the native peoples of that land and to spread Christianity — in fact, St. Mary's order opened the first educational institute for girls in the whole of North America. At the age of seven, she had a dream which she described thus:

> In my sleep one night, it seemed to me that I was in a schoolyard…. Suddenly the skies opened, and Our Lord emerged, advancing toward me! When Jesus neared me, I stretched out my arms to embrace Him. Jesus embraced me affectionately and asked me: "Do you want to belong to Me?" I answered, "Yes."[4]

And belong to him she did. After she had been widowed, she felt such a powerful call to the religious life that she gave her eleven-year-old son to the care of her sister in order to pursue it. He wasn't happy about it — in fact, he tried to break into her monastery to be reunited

3 William Lawson SJ, *Blessed Rafaela Maria Porras (1850–1925)* (Dublin: Clonmore and Reynolds), 135.

4 Scottish Order of Saint Margaret Friars Mendicant, "Saint of the Day: 02 June 2013," https://warder5150.wordpress.com/2013/06/02/saint-of-the-day-02-june-2013/ (accessed May 27, 2017).

with his mother. In later life, however, he became a Benedictine monk, and his mother's first biographer.

Another vision, this time involving our Blessed Mother as well as our Lord, convinced St. Mary that her destiny was to go to the New World. Sponsorship from a wealthy Frenchwoman provided the necessary funds, and with two other Ursuline nuns and a Jesuit priest, she set out for Quebec. There, she set to work giving both the daughters of French settlers, and the daughters of the various native Canadian tribes, a spiritual and practical education. She composed dictionaries and catechisms in several native Canadian languages. St. Mary of the Incarnation died at the age of seventy-one, and was canonized by Pope Francis in 2014.

God speaks to all of us and helps us to discern our path in life, whether that comes through a miraculous intervention, a "Eureka moment" of inspiration, or a gradual process of reflection. God speaks, but do we listen? The lives of the saints are an inspiring record of those who cried "Yes!" to the request God made of them.

Boldness

St. Josemaría Escrivá ✳ *St. John Paul II*
St. Thérèse of Lisieux ✳ *St. Maximilian Kolbe*

OUR LORD ADMIRED AUDACITY. TIME AND AGAIN, in the gospels, we see him praising people for their boldness in making requests of him. Sometimes he even denied their requests at first, only to (apparently) change his mind when they were not put off by the refusal. Of course, our Lord knew what was in everybody's heart. Doubtless he turned them down at first *knowing* that they would not be put off, and that their persistence would be a lesson to millions of others in the future.

Perhaps the most famous instance of Jesus rewarding persistence is the story of the Canaanite woman:

> Leaving that place, Jesus withdrew to the region of Tyre and Sidon. A Canaanite woman from that vicinity came to him, crying out, "Lord, Son of David, have mercy on me! My daughter is demon-possessed and suffering terribly."
>
> Jesus did not answer a word. So his disciples came to him and urged him, "Send her away, for she keeps crying out after us."
>
> He answered, "I was sent only to the lost sheep of Israel."
>
> The woman came and knelt before him. "Lord, help me!" she said.
>
> He replied, "It is not right to take the children's bread and toss it to the dogs."
>
> "Yes it is, Lord," she said. "Even the dogs eat the crumbs that fall from their master's table."

Then Jesus said to her, "Woman, you have great faith! Your request is granted." And her daughter was healed at that moment. (Matthew 15:21–28)

One notable characteristic of the lives of the saints is that (to use a modern phrase) they *think big*. They have extravagant visions, visions that others dismiss as pie-in-the-sky—yet, amazingly often, they bring these visions to fulfillment. A saint that we have already discussed, St. Josemaría Escrivá, is a good example of this characteristic. His biographer, Salvador Bernal, dedicates a full chapter to St. Josemaría's daring. He writes:

Pedro Rocamora met Msgr. Escrivá de Belaguer around 1928 and, although Rocamora did not join Opus Dei, he felt right from the start a deep respect and affection for that young priest, Don Josemaria, who trusted him as a true friend and who, shortly after the birth of the Work, talked to him about his "foundational" ideas. These struck Rocamora as being too ambitious: "He expressed them with such simplicity and he was so convinced they would succeed that I was just amazed." Though he admired Don Josemaria, he "could not hide a certain skepticism regarding such projects. They seemed too big, beautiful indeed, but impossible to achieve."

Even those who had faith in—as well as friendship for—the Founder of Opus Dei felt a sense of vertigo when he spoke to them about the future, because his "dreams" had no human foundation whatsoever. This same impression of vertigo—produced by Don Josemaria's faith and confidence in God—is, as we saw, what remains in the memories of the members of the Women's Section of the Work when they recall how he talked about the tasks their Section would undertake in the future. He always insisted that the most important thing would be the personal apostolate of each member, which was something impossible for gauge or measure; but the zeal they put into their personal apostolate would give rise in its turn to the most varied initiatives; farming schools for country girls, centers for the professional training of women, halls of residence for college students, activities in the field of fashion.... When those few women expressed their amazement, the Founder of Opus Dei urged them to see that the only thing they need was to trust in God; the Lord wanted all this to come about, and so it would be God who would push his Work ahead.

It would be pointed out that, from the very beginning, Don Josemaria had in his mind and nurtured in his heart many activities that would not become reality till years later.... Professor Jimenez Vargas stresses that "when, nearly twenty years later, I was told about the plans for the University of Navarre, I was not in the least surprised because the ideas went back for a long time." He adds, "those ideas were the same as I had heard from him in 1933."[1]

The Pope who canonized St. Josemaría Escrivá, John Paul II, was himself a saint who exemplified boldness. "Be not afraid!" was one of his mottoes, and one that he used in his first speech as Pope in 1978. Even in the making of saints, he was a model of boldness. He canonized 482 people, and beatified over 1,300. (Some of these were collective canonizations or beatifications, such as the eighty-five martyrs of England and Wales who were beatified on 22 November 1987.) He beatified and canonized more people than all the Popes in the four centuries before him put together.

Some people have criticized St. John Paul for this extravagance, arguing that he trivialized sainthood by making too many saints and blesseds. I don't think Our Lord would disapprove of it any more than he disapproved of the extravagance of the woman who poured ointment over him.

St. John Paul the Second is also remarkable for the breadth of his travels. He visited one hundred and twenty nine countries during his pontificate. A press release from Reuters after his death estimated that, as Pope, he had traveled more than 775,000 miles — more than three

---

1 Salvador Bernal, *Msgr. Josemaría Escrivá de Belaguer: A Profile of the Founder of Opus Dei* (Dublin: Veritas, 1977), 183–185.

times the distance between the earth and the moon. (Some people mistakenly think he was the first Pope to travel the world. However, his near-predecessor Pope Paul VI started the trend, becoming the first ever Pope to fly on a plane in 1967.)

St. John Paul II

St. John Paul was a missionary Pope. In his encyclical *Redemptoris Missio*, he asserted the missionary nature of the Catholic Church:

The mission of Christ the Redeemer, which is entrusted to the Church, is still very far from completion. As the second millennium after Christ's coming draws to an end, an overall view of the human race shows that this mission is still only beginning and that we must commit ourselves wholeheartedly to its service. It is the Spirit who impels us to proclaim the great works of God: "For if I preach the Gospel, that gives me no ground for boasting. For necessity is laid upon me. Woe to me if I do not preach the Gospel!" (1 Cor 9:16)

In the name of the whole Church, I sense an urgent duty to repeat this cry of St. Paul. From the beginning of my Pontificate I have chosen to travel to the ends of the earth in order to show this missionary concern. My direct contact with peoples who do not know Christ has convinced me even more of the urgency of missionary activity.[2]

"The urgency of missionary activity" is a theme dear to the heart of many saints, as we will see presently.

When it comes to the boldness of saints, we cannot exclude a story from the life of St. Thérèse of Lisieux (1873–1897), the most popular saint of the contemporary world. This French Carmelite sister was the originator of "the Little Way," a form of spirituality which emphasizes a child-like acceptance of our own littleness, and a desire to perform the acts of everyday life with great love.

But even though the theatre of her life was small, St. Thérèse had great ambitions in her own way, as this charming anecdote from her childhood shows:

One day, Leonie [her sister], thinking she was too big to be playing any longer with dolls, came to us with a basket filled with dresses and pretty pieces for making others; her doll was resting on top. "Here, my little sisters, choose; I'm giving you all this." Celine stretched out her hand and took a little ball of wool that pleased her. After a moment's reflection, I stretched out mine saying: "I choose all!" and I took the basket without further ceremony.

2 St. John Paul II, *Redemptoris Video: On the Permanent Validity of the Church's Missionary Mandate.* http://w2.vatican.va/content/john-paul-ii/en/encyclicals/documents/hf_jp-ii_enc_07121990_redemptoris-missio.html (accessed May 27, 2017).

Those who witnessed the scene saw nothing wrong and even Celine herself didn't dream of complaining (besides, she had all sorts of toys, her godfather gave her lots of presents, and Louise found ways of getting her everything she desired).

St. Thérèse of Lisieux

This little incident of my childhood is a summary of my whole life; later on when perfection was set before me, I understood that to become a saint one had to suffer much, seek out always the most perfect thing to do, and forget self. I understood, too, that there were many degrees of perfection and each soul was free to respond to the advances of Our Lord, to do little or much for

Him, in a word, to choose amongst the sacrifices He was asking. Then, as in the days of my childhood, I cried out: "My God, 'I choose all'! I don't want to be a saint by halves, I'm not afraid to suffer for You, I fear only one thing; to keep my own will; so take it, for 'I choose all' that You will!"[3]

Boldness was to be a feature of St. Thérèse's life. In fact, when she was told she was too young to enter a Carmelite Convent, she took the case to her local bishop...and then to the Pope himself! In an audience with Pope Leo XIII, despite being told that she was not supposed to speak, she asked His Holiness to intervene in her case, and persevered when his answer was non-committal. Eventually, she had to be carried away from the Pope by two guards.

Although she did not get the reply she was seeking from the Holy Father, she did ultimately get permission from her bishop to enter the convent at age fifteen. Although she died at the age of twenty-four, the impact of her autobiography *Story of a Soul* led her to be called "the greatest saint of modern times" by Pope Pius X, and to be proclaimed a Doctor of the Church by Pope John Paul II in 1997. (A Doctor of the Church is a writer whose writings have had a great influence on the whole Church.)

A story very similar to the story of St. Thérèse and the basket comes from the life of St. Maximilian Kolbe (1894–1941), a Polish Franciscan whose life was full of extraordinary initiatives, and who died in a Nazi extermination camp when he chose to take the place of a man scheduled for execution.

When he was a boy, St. Maximilian had a vision of the Blessed Mother:

That night I asked the Mother of God what was to become of me. Then she came to me holding two crowns, one white, the other red. She asked if I was willing to accept either of these crowns. The white one meant that I should persevere in purity,

---

3 St. Thérèse of Lisieux, *Story of a Soul: The Autobiography of St. Thérèse of Lisieux* (Washington DC: ICS Publications, 1972), 27.

and the red that I should become a martyr. I said that I would accept them both.[4]

St. Maximilian Kolbe

When he was a seminarian, St. Maximilian Kolbe came up with a bold plan of his own, as biographer Desmond Forristal records:

4 Mary Craig, *Blessed Maximilian Kolbe—Priest Hero of a Death Camp.* http://www. ewtn.com/library/MARY/kolbe2.htm (accessed May 27, 2017).

The plan which Maximilian had been resolving in his mind since the beginning of the year was nothing less than this: the conversion of the world through the intercession of the Immaculate. The idea had come to him one morning while he was at prayer and having thought it over he went to consult his confessor and spiritual director. The confessor may have smiled inwardly at this simplistic and naive master-plan but he did nothing to discourage the young man. He may have discerned in him not just the generosity and enthusiasm of youth, but also some foreshadowing of that tenacity and fixity of purpose which were to become so marked in his later life. In time to come the young man would find out how grand general schemes can come to grief on the practical problems of daily life; but he would have the natural and supernatural resources to deal with those problems and triumphantly overcome them.[5]

The rather far-fetched idea of one seminarian turned out to be anything but a pipe dream; a hundred years later, the Militia of the Immaculate continue to flourish all over the world, with about three million members. Members make a personal act of consecration to the Virgin Mary and wear the Miraculous Medal. Its website describes the association in these words: "The aim of the MI is to win the whole world for Christ through the Immaculata, Mother of God and of the Church." All this from an initial meeting of seven seminarians, not all of whom were particularly enthusiastic.

St. Maximilian, however, went from bold initiative to bold initiative. From his friary, he printed a magazine called *The Knight of the Immaculate*. It grew so successful that the friary became crowded with the printing presses needed for its publication. Eventually, St. Maximilian set up a monastery of his own in which it could be printed—Niepokalanów, "the City of the Immaculate Mother of God." So many friars were attracted to this work that over 700 men were working there before World War Two, and over 750,000 copies *of The Knight of the Immaculate* were being printed.

---

5 Desmond Forristal, *Maximilian of Auschwitz* (Dublin: Ward River Press, 1982), 44.

St. Maximilian still wasn't satisfied. He wanted to take the *Knight* to the Far East. Forristal describes how he did this:

> To the modern mind, the five travellers would seem to have been exceptionally ill-prepared for the journey. In those days missionaries did not undergo the rigorous training and orientation that are considered essential today; it was time enough to start learning the local language and customs when they arrived at their destination. But these five were not even clear what the destination was. All they knew was that they were going to build cities and publish writings for the glory of God and the salvation of souls. They hoped to be in Shanghai in mid-April, which would give them two weeks before the beginning of May, traditionally the month of Mary. It would be very fitting if they could honour her during that month by publishing the first issue of The Knight in Chinese or Japanese or both. The fact that they knew not a word of these languages did not bother them at all. If the Immaculate wanted it, it would come to pass.[6]

St. Maximilian was not very successful in China, but the monastery which he built in Japan still continues today.

Of course, this saint's crowning moment came during the Second World War, when (along with four others of his monastery) he was arrested and sent to Auschwitz. As previously mentioned, he voluntarily took the place of a man condemned to death by starvation in an underground bunker. The man himself survived the extermination camp and died more than fifty years later.

St. Kolbe was put in a cell with nine other men, who were denied all food and water until they died of starvation. He led them in prayers and hymns as they succumbed one by one. After two weeks, only Fr. Maximilian was left alive, and his death had to be hastened with a lethal injection.

The story of his martyrdom is unforgettable. But even if he had died in bed of old age, St. Maximilian would have been an amazing

6 Ibid., 89.

example of Christian boldness. Consider that, when the idea of consecrating the world to Mary came to him, he was a simple seminarian. Learning the vocation of being a priest might have been expected to be enough for him. But no; even at that age, even at that stage in his development, this ardent soul was dreaming of ways to convert the entire world. Reading the story of this saint, we see someone who was not only seized with zeal, but with a divine *impatience*. He struggled with sickness at many stages of his life, and his brothers convinced him to recuperate only with great difficulty; he always had some new project "on the go." Considering that Christianity was already nineteen centuries old at this point, and that Christians have no idea when our Lord will return, one might ask: what was St. Maximilian's hurry? Of course, the answer to that is that each of us only has one lifetime to say "yes" to Christ. Millions of men and women are passing through the portals of birth and death every day; it is these men and women, the men and women of our own time, whom we are called to lead to their Savior. Tomorrow may be too late. We have great need for boldness!

In Other People's Eyes

St. Charles of Mount Argus ✳ *St. Damian of Molokai*
St. Bernadette of Lourdes ✳ *St. Mother Teresa of Calcutta*
St. Gemma Galgani ✳ *Blessed John Sullivan S.J.*

ONE OF THE MOST FASCINATING THINGS ABOUT
the saints is their "aura," the impression they made on other people.
The Bible tells us that "If any man is in Christ, he is a new creature"
(2 Corinthians 5:17). The very presence of the saints tends to have an
uplifting effect on others.

The perspective of others is valuable, because saints usually have a
very harsh view of themselves. One example of this truth is an anecdote
from the life of St. Charles of Mount Argus (1821–1893) — a Dutch
Passionist priest who served in a Dublin monastery and won a reputation for great holiness:

> He would often be seen standing at a window from which could
> be seen the brickworks, which filled the sky with a red glow: "Oh,
> the sufferings of the damned, and I deserve them for all my sins!
> Oh God, be merciful to me, a sinner!"[1]

When we read such self-castigation, so very common in the words
of the saints, we may be tempted to think that the saints are too hard
on themselves. But reader, consider; what if the saints were right, and
it is we who are *far too easy* on ourselves? How much more we need
the mercy of Jesus Christ and the grace of the sacraments!

Self-criticism is by no means the only criticism the saints come
in for. In fact, it seems a very common experience of holy men and

---

1 Fr. Christopher C.R., *Father Charles of Mount Argus* (Dublin: M.H. Gill, 1955), 97.

women that they encounter opposition — even opposition from good people.

Upon the death of St. Damian of Molakai (1840–1889), a Belgian priest who worked for years amongst the lepers of Hawaii (and who eventually contracted leprosy himself), a highly critical letter appeared in an American newspaper, written by a Dr. Hyde, who was himself a Christian missionary and a man of many charitable works. He wrote:

> We who knew the man are surprised at the extravagant newspaper laudations, as if he was a most saintly philanthropist. The simple truth is he was a coarse dirty man, headstrong and bigoted.... Others have done much for the lepers, our own ministers, the government physicians, and so forth, but never with the Catholic idea of meriting eternal life.[2]

This letter (which was never meant to be made public) was answered by a letter from Robert Louis Stevenson, the author of *Treasure Island* and other famous works, who had spent time on the leper colony where Fr. Damien worked (though the two had never met). Stevenson defended Fr. Damien in the most impassioned terms, and did not refrain from pouring considerable scorn on the head of the somewhat unfortunate Dr. Hyde. (The reader may be wondering whether this Dr. Hyde was the inspiration for the alter ego of Dr. Jekyll in Stevenson's story, *The Strange Case of Dr. Jekyll and Mr. Hyde*. It would make a good story, but the answer is no — this controversy occurred after the publication of that tale.)

This was not a unique reaction to St. Damien. One of his biographers, May Quinlan, describes the reservations many of his contemporaries felt about him:

> The lofty idealism that always dominated his scheme of social reform, and the strength of will which enabled him to impose upon the leper colony a standard of ethics higher than that of

---

2 May Quinlan, *Father Damien of Molokai* (London: MacDonald and Evans, 1914), 98.

the majority of his fellow workers, postulated a type of man calculated to grate upon the susceptibilities of less noble minds. His ways were not their ways. His idiosyncrasies annoyed them. His forceful character got on their nerves.

St. Damian of Molokai

And what did they say of him — those men who during the latter years of his life, shared with him the burdens of local government? "A difficult man to work with," said one; "a good man, but very officious," said a third; "brusque and overbearing" said a fourth... while all alike condemned his social methods — his orphanages, said they, were ill-managed, over-crowded and ill-kept.

So, if you are smarting from unfair criticism despite your best efforts, and even if this criticism comes from good people, you may comfort yourself that canonized saints have had their critics.

Let us consider, however, some of the more positive impressions that saints have made on those who met them. Here is an example of the impression made by St. Bernadette of Lourdes on a fellow Sister of Charity (the "purificator" alluded to is a cloth used to wipe the chalice after Communion):

> When she was a sacristan, another sister, Sister Vincent Garros, helped her with her work: "One day I wanted to handle a purificator. Bernadette stopped me and said: 'You've not got that far yet!' And I watched her take this purificator with great reverence and put it back into the burse. You would have thought she was praying while handling these objects, so great was the reverence with which she treated them."[3]

This attentiveness to little things — "small things done with great love," as Mother Teresa said — seems to have been a feature of most (perhaps all) of the saints. It is an approach which is urged on us in Scripture, too: "Let all that you do be done in love" (1 Corinthians 16:14). Such carefulness is an extremely attractive feature, by any standard — sacred or secular. Have you ever noticed how pleasant it is to watch *anything* done carefully and lovingly — whether by a proud housewife laying a table, a chess player setting up the board, a mother wiping her baby's face, or a maker of model airplanes delicately putting some small piece into place? The smallest actions of people in such a frame of mind are deliberate, meaningful, expressive — the entire person is concentrated in the gesture. From accounts of the saints, it would seem a common feature that they invest their entire being into each word

3 Francis Trochu, *Saint Bernadette Soubirous* (London: Longmans, Green and Co., 1957), 305.

and act, as St. Bernadette did with the purificator. This is especially notable in the case of saintly priests celebrating Mass — those who witnessed St. Josemaría Escrivá or St. Padre Pio celebrating the liturgy were often greatly exalted by the spectacle.

St. Bernadette Soubirous

To return to St. Bernadette, here is another fascinating account of the impression she made. Crowds came to witness her meetings with Our Lady (although only she could see the apparition) and one young man who came to scoff, has left a very moving account of his change of heart:

Spontaneously, we men who were present uncovered our heads and bent our knees, like the humblest woman. The time for argument was past, and we, like all those present at this heavenly scene, were gazing from the ecstatic girl to the rock, and from the rock to the ecstatic [girl]. We saw nothing, we heard nothing, needless to say; but what we could see and comprehend was that a conversation had begun between the mysterious Lady and the child whom we had before our eyes....

It was a most solemn hour of my life! I was thrown almost into a delirium of madness by the thought that a cynical, sneering, self-satisfied fellow like me had been permitted to come so close to the Queen of Heaven.[4]

Of course, this magnetism is not confined to saints who have had supernatural revelations. Here is an "outsider's view" of one of the twentieth century's most celebrated saints, St. Edith Stein (1891–1942)—a German Jewish woman who gave up a brilliant career in philosophy to become a Carmelite nun, and who died in a Nazi extermination camp. We see again that saints seem to carry their own special "aura" around with them.

I saw the Fraulein Doktor for the first time from my classroom window as she went across the court into the seminar with a pile of books under her arm. I was so struck by her personality—though I did not know in the least who she was—that I have never forgotten that first impression. Later on I entered St. Magdalena's and therefore had the chance of going to the lectures which she gave the Sisters. Later still I got to know her personally and spent many happy hours with her, and she gave me Latin lessons and some instructions in English and French. When it was fine we used to meet in the convent garden—a flag at her window, which I could see from the noviciate corridor, let me know that she was waiting for me out of doors. With very few

4 Ibid., 96–97.

words—just by her personality and everything which emanated from her—she set me on my way, not only in my studies but in my whole moral life. With her you felt that you were in an atmosphere of everything noble, pure and sublime which simply carried you up with it.

To see her praying in church, where she often knelt motionless for hours at a time, besides the times of the services, was an impressive sermon. And with it all she was so open and simple. There was always great goings-on in her room before Christmas. There was a surprise for everyone in any way connected with her, all beautifully wrapped up. And what big parcels found their way secretly to the poor in the town![5]

Another perspective on the same saint:

When I saw her for the first time in a corner of the entrance to Beuron, her appearance and attitude made an impression on me which I can only compare with that of the pictures of the *ecclesia orans* [praying figures] in the oldest ecclesiastical art of the Catacombs. Apart from the arms uplifted in prayer, everything about her was reminiscent of the Christian archetype. And this was no mere chance fancy. She was in truth a type of that ecclesia, standing in the world of time and yet apart from it, and knowing nothing else, in the depths of her union with Christ, but the Lord's words: *For them do I sanctify myself; that they also may be sanctified in truth.*[6]

Perhaps the appeal of such pen-pictures, such glimpses into the everyday personalities of the saints, is that they remind us that sanctity is lived out moment by moment. Most of us have generous moods, pious moods, irreverent moods, giddy moods, and so forth—we might try to live a holy life every minute of the day for a week or two, and then become tired of the effort, or become absorbed in a different mood.

---

5 Sister Teresia de Spiritu Sancto, O.D.C., *Edith Stein* (London: Sheed and Ward, 1950), 75.
6 Ibid., 85.

It is startling (and inspiring, and challenging) to realize that this isn't inevitable — that there are people who never stop trying to live a life of holiness, every minute of the day and every day of the year.

One of the more charming glimpses into the lovability of a saint comes to us from the Acts of the Apostles, when we see St. Paul bidding farewell to the Ephesians for the last time, before he goes to Jerusalem:

> "Now I know that none of you among whom I have gone about preaching the kingdom will ever see me again. Therefore, I declare to you today that I am innocent of the blood of any of you. For I have not hesitated to proclaim to you the whole will of God. Keep watch over yourselves and all the flock of which the Holy Spirit has made you overseers. Be shepherds of the church of God, which he bought with his own blood. I know that after I leave, savage wolves will come in among you and will not spare the flock. Even from your own number men will arise and distort the truth in order to draw away disciples after them. So be on your guard! Remember that for three years I never stopped warning each of you night and day with tears."
>
> When Paul had finished speaking, he knelt down with all of them and prayed. They all wept as they embraced him and kissed him. (Acts 20:25–30, 36–37)

In his letters, St. Paul so often seems like a stern patriarch, frequently chiding and rebuking. But we see from this brief description that the great apostle inspired affection as well as reverence. For once, we see him as a man, rather than a force of nature.

I have already mentioned St. Josemaría Escrivá, the founder of Opus Dei, several times. Many people have recorded the impression he made upon them, and they speak with one voice of a kind of holy charisma. Victor Frankl, the Holocaust survivor who wrote *Man's Search for Meaning*, had this to say about St. Josemaría:

> If I am to say what it was that fascinated me particularly about his personality, it was above all the refreshing serenity which

emanated from him and warmed the whole conversation. Next the unbelievable rhythm with which his thought flows, and finally his amazing capacity for getting into immediate contact with those he is speaking to.[7]

This final quality — a "capacity for getting into immediate contact with those he is speaking to" — is one that is often mentioned in descriptions of the saints. A characteristic of saints seems to be their real and unfeigned interest in every human being they meet.

Returning to St. Josemaría Escrivá, his biographer Salvador Bernal stresses his joyfulness, naturalness, and normality:

All who have met him and been with him, even for a few moments, are unanimous in singling out his happiness. His peaceful, open look was cordially welcoming. He was a man of God who overflowed with attraction and human warmth. He infused peace and cheerfulness, serenity, contentment and the desire to serve others.

"I can think of no-one," Manual Aznar wrote a few days later, "who combined as intimately as he did, and with such spontaneity and such admirable naturalness, the natural with the supernatural, God with man and man with God." He accomplished that hardest of tasks of keeping supernatural inspirations present in the midst of the tiniest trivialities of human existence, and did so without apparent effort, with no jarring as the yearning for higher things engaged with reality here below.

He lived for God, and was also marvellously human. To carry out the Work entrusted to him by Our Lord, he received gifts that made him humanly attractive, and, at the same time, surprising, since people often expect a "founder" to be somewhat "special" or different. "I had to keep making acts of faith, to remind myself that I was in the presence of the Founder of Opus Dei. He is so straightforward and easy to get on with," was the comment

7 Salvador Bernal, *Msgr. Josemaría Escrivá de Belaguer: A Profile of the Founder of Opus Dei* (Dublin: Veritas, 1977), 156.

made by a priest from Jaen when he met him in Pozoalbero, near Jerez de la Frontera (Spain), on a November day in 1972. Another priest remarked on "how naturally he hides the depth of his spirituality." But, he added: "It just bubbles out. He can't hide God's presence within him."[8]

When we read such accounts of the personalities of the saints, we may feel a tremendous sense of regret at how far we are from such an ideal. We go through so many moods, often in the one day; by turns petty, irritable, friendly, whimsical, melancholy, sour, enthusiastic, and so on. Each of us might ask: Which is the real *me*? Why is my personality dispersed amongst so many different roles? In the lives of the saints, we see (to once again use this word) the kind of *wholeness* to which we should all aspire — and to which we *can* all aspire, even if our progress towards this ideal is slow and never completed.

Here is a description from Monsignor Peter Wolf of St. Mother Teresa of Calcutta. Mother Teresa, as most people will know, was the Albanian nun who founded the Missionaries of Charity, an order which engages in many charitable endeavors. She was one of the most famous Catholics of the last century:

> She stood before me in her white Sari with its blue border, much smaller than I had imagined her. She was very attentive as she faced me. I had the feeling that at the same time as she was speaking to me she was praying. The Rosary slipped constantly through her bony fingers. She was wholly with God and yet wholly with the people before her. I joyfully told her of a young student who had told me of her wish to join Mother Teresa's community.
>
> After our conversation in the office, we went to the house chapel in the Spiritual Centre of the *Katholikentag*, which had been set up in the Borromeus College. Hardly had she caught sight of the tabernacle than she sank to her knees; with all her senses she was directed towards HIM…. Afterwards I accompanied her

through the house to the entrance opening onto the street. People constantly arrived who simply wanted to touch her clothes. It seemed to me like in the Gospel when Jesus went through the streets and people wanted to touch him.[9]

Again, we see the motif of attentiveness, of wholeness: "she was wholly with God and yet wholly with the people before her." And we see another motif which is often mentioned in connection with the saints: the sense that the saint is always praying, even when he or she is talking, working, or doing other activities. This is a fulfilment of St. Paul's injunction to "pray without ceasing" (1 Thessalonians 5:17). The term "recollection" is often applied to this quality—the *Catholic Encyclopedia* describes recollection as "attention to the presence of God in the soul."

Another saint who made a particularly vivid impression on those around her was St. Gemma Galgani (1878–1903), an Italian mystic who died at the age of twenty-three. St. Gemma is rather like St. Padre Pio in many respects. Both of these saints seem to have walked straight out of the Middle Ages into the modern era. Both were stigmatists—that is, people upon whose bodies the wounds of Jesus on the Cross (the *stigmata*) miraculously appeared. Both of them communicated with Our Lord, his Blessed Mother, and the citizens of heaven as familiarly as if they were calling them on the telephone. (St. Gemma, endearingly, addressed Our Lady as "Mom.")

For much of her life she lived with a family by the name Giannini. The lady of the house had this to say about her:

"With Gemma at my side," she used to say, "I rest, I find myself refreshed, and no longer feel the weight of my work, nor the bitterness of disagreeables." And then she was wont to add: "What account shall not I have to give to God, if I don't value the treasure He has given me, in this angelic creature, and profit thereby for my soul's good!"

9 Msgr. Peter Wolf DD, *Mother Teresa: Encounter with a Saint*, 2016. http://www.schoenstatt.org/en/francis/2016/08/mother-teresa-encounter-with-a-saint/ (accessed May 27, 2017).

And as this lady thought, so likewise thought all the other members of the family, as well on the first day they came to possess Gemma as on the last when heaven took her from them. The mother of that family bears testimony by letter as follows:

> Of our Gemma I have only to say, that the most extraordinary and wonderful things continue more and more to happen to her; and when I look at her I seem to behold in her something that is not of this world. What a happiness to have lived thus with such an angel! A world of things would not be enough to give you an idea of what goes on in her. She is an angel in human form, and that expresses all.[10]

A priest who knew her had this to say:

> To know and to admire this dear child, so adorned with virtue and rich in the gifts of God, was one and the same thing. I was charmed by her extraordinary ingenuousness, which seemed almost to challenge her more than ordinary intelligence. Full of admiration I observed her continually, and during the whole time that she was in our house I had constant opportunities of remarking not only her scrupulous exactness in every duty, but also her denial of her own will and her exercise of every virtue.
>
> Her virtues were practiced with such promptness, diligence and calmness, that they seemed to have become part of her nature. I admired in particular her spirit of recollection and union with God. Even in the midst of domestic occupations of the most distracting kind she was always seen as if absorbed in God, and in continual meditation. This did not hinder her from attending with great care to whatever she was doing. The fervor of her piety seemed to radiate from her person, especially from her eyes which she was wont to keep modestly downcast. Indeed

---

10 Venerable Reverend Germanus C.P., *The Life of the Servant of God Gemma Galgani. An Italian Maid of Lucca.* http://www.stgemmagalgani.com/p/the-life-of-saint-gemma-galgani.html (accessed 27 May 2017).

I must confess that on her glancing at me I felt so impressed that I could not look her in the face.[11]

Even photographs of St. Gemma convey the magnetism, holiness and directness of her character. We are not surprised to read, in the reports of those who knew her, of the fragrance of her personality.

St. Gemma Galgani

And yet St. Gemma, too, experienced ridicule and hostility from some members of the community, even from some members of her own family. Her personality was so simple, and her reluctance to draw attention to herself so strong, that many people thought she was lacking in intelligence.

11 Ibid.

An Irish saint beatified as I was writing this, Fr. John Sullivan SJ (1861–1933), a convert from Anglicanism, is another saint who made a powerful impression on those around him. He was the son of the Lord Chancellor of Ireland (the highest position in the Irish judicial system, before Ireland won its independence from England). After a distinguished period in university, he commenced a career in law. Wealthy, intelligent, and handsome, he had all the ingredients for a rich life in the world. But two events intervened — the death of his father and a visit to Mount Athos, the Orthodox monastery in Greece. (Greek Orthodoxy is one branch of Eastern Orthodoxy, a form of Christianity quite similar to Catholicism, but which does not accept the authority of the Pope. The Eastern Orthodox churches have been split from the Roman Catholic Church since the eleventh century, though hopes for reunification continue.)

John contemplated becoming an Orthodox monk but eventually converted to Catholicism, astonishing his family, as he had never shown any special interest in religion. He joined the Jesuits and became a teacher in the famous Jesuit school at Clongowes in Kildare, in the east of Ireland. He was not a good teacher, but his pupils revered him for his evident holiness. He became known as "the saint on a bicycle" for his readiness to visit anyone who required the ministrations of a priest. Whenever Fr. John entered a house, his first question was: "Are there any sick here?" If the response was, "None, thank God," he would reprove the person who replied this way — the sick, he said, were a blessing to any house. Miraculous healings were attributed to him even in his lifetime.

We have some memorable descriptions of Fr. Sullivan:

> He was a most pleasant companion on walks. His wide experience of life, his cultured mind, knowledge of the classics and lives of the saints, and his constant union with God, all enabled him to be religiously interesting and entertainingly spiritual. He spoke frequently of St. Monica and St. Augustine, to both of whom he had a marked devotion. He had a rather melancholy voice, especially when reading or preaching, and his spirituality was

tinged, I think, with a gentle sadness that resulted from his clear realization of the sorrow that the sins of men gave to the Sacred Heart of our Lord. He spoke easily on this subject and on the Passion, which was never far from his thoughts. Occasionally, in those days, he told an amusing story, and when he did, his face at the climax would light up with an apologetic smile, his eyes would just for a moment glance keenly at you; then his voice would change to a deeper tone, and his hand would be drawn across his eyes as if to obliterate his folly in recounting the story.[12]

A religious sister who attended one of his retreats had this to say:

It was the character and demeanour of the man that impressed us all. One could not come into contact with him and fail to realize that he was truly a man closely united to God. In his manner of acting and speaking he seemed to belong to another world.[13]

Again we hear that description: "Seemed to belong to another world," just as St. Gemma was described as "something that is not of this world." These descriptions echo the traditional Christian principle that we should be "in the world but not of the world," a principle that takes its source from the Last Supper discourse in the gospel of John, where Jesus says of his disciples: "They do not belong to the world any more than I belong to the world" (John 17:16).

"Tell me who your friends are, and I'll tell you who you are" is a proverb with a lot of truth to it. The same applies to heroes. If our heroes are delinquent rock stars, or egotistical movie actors, or "bad boy" characters in some TV series, we can hardly help picking up some of their self-absorption or their contempt for others. We will copy that sneer, that swagger, that saucy look which we associate with these glamorous individuals. Even without realizing it, we may find ourselves aping them. Sometimes we will mimic their mannerisms

---

12 Fergal McGrath S.J., *Father John Sullivan S.J.* (London: Longman's, Green and Co., 1941), 81.
13 Ibid., 171.

while adding the supposedly saving grace of irony — but of course, irony does not mitigate the corrosive effect that this influence has on our characters and our view of the world.

All day long, every single day of our lives, we are surrounded by the tawdry glamour of pop culture. We can no more avoid encountering it than we can avoid inhaling car fumes on a busy road. But one way in which can *counter* such tawdry glamour is to steep ourselves in the *holy glamour* of the saints — by praying to them, certainly, but also by reading about them and contemplating them. We should contemplate especially the way in which they make virtue (rather than vice) so very attractive…or even so very *exciting*. If we make friends with the saints, we can hardly help being ever more drawn to sanctity — and to Jesus.

70

Mortification

St. Junipero Serra ✳ St. Rose of Lima ✳ St. Paul of Tarsus
St. Catherine Ricci ✳ St. John Paul II ✳ St. Josemaría Escrivá
St. Mary of the Incarnation ✳ St. John Berchmans
St. Jean Vianney ✳ St. Francis of Assisi

THE SINGLE CHARACTERISTIC OF THE SAINTS THAT baffles the modern world the most must be their enthusiasm for mortification. In fact, the whole idea of mortifying the body is one that tends to baffle us today. Even Christians view it with some coolness at best, and often with outright distaste. But what exactly *is* mortification? The *Catholic Encyclopedia* describes mortification thus: "One of the methods which Christian asceticism employs in training the soul to virtuous and holy living." When Jesus went into the wilderness to fast for forty days and nights, he was practicing mortification. When Catholics abstain from eating meat on Good Friday, they are practicing mortification.

Contemporary society—or much of it, anyway—has got into its head that Christianity hates the body and pleasure. H.L. Mencken describes puritanism as: "The haunting suspicion that someone, somewhere, is having a good time." The witticism, many would think, could just as well apply to Christianity in general.

But Christianity does not teach that the body or pleasure is evil. Indeed, Scripture very often uses wine, marriage, and feasting as symbols of Heaven. Various heresies throughout Christian history have sought to condemn the body and the physical world as evil—and, invariably, the Catholic Church has denounced them. The heresy of gnosticism, which I mentioned previously, is the prime example. (We still have gnostics with us, though they tend to drape themselves in the banner of the "New Age.") Against all this, orthodox Christianity has always held to the clear teaching of the Bible: "Everything God created is good" (1 Timothy 4:4).

However, human beings have a powerful habit of taking something good and doing something bad with it. Wine is good, but getting drunk on it is not. Sex is good, but adultery is not. Intelligence is good, but using it to plan a robbery is not. As well as this, sometimes we simply become too attached to pleasures or other good things, which draw us away from things that are more important. You can see this (for instance) in the life of the workaholic, who neglects his family and health in order to devote ever more time and effort to his job.

The irony is that people in modern society have no problem in denying their pleasures or disciplining their bodies when their goal is a worldly one. For instance, see how physically fit and toned many young people keep themselves today; going to the gym is an essential part of their routine. Of course, this is not a bad thing—it is good to be healthy and fit. The reason I mention it is because it shows that mortification *per se* is not a bewildering idea to our culture. We don't mind sacrifice or endurance for the sake of the body, or for the sake of our careers. More altruistically, many of us can make quite significant sacrifices (such as cycling rather than driving) for the sake of the environment. But somehow such sacrifices are seen as morbid when the beneficiary is the soul.

On the other hand, our culture can often be quite *fascinated* by mortification. This displays itself in surprising ways. Reader, have you ever experienced a lengthy power cut? If you have, the chances are that you have rather fond memories of it. When the electricity fails, people are thrown onto their own imaginations; telling stories, playing charades, making shadow puppets on the wall by the light of a candle. It may seem a trivial example, but it shows how a deprivation can actually enrich us.

The experience of a heavy snowfall is similar. Of course, schoolchildren like to get the day off school, but even for adults, who are usually more seriously inconvenienced, snowfalls or other adverse weather conditions can be a break in the routine, an opportunity to bond with others, and a subject of conversation for future days and weeks (or even *years*, in the case of really bad weather).

People may also wax nostalgic about deprivations of the past — such as when they had to stand in long cinema queues, before the advent of multiplex cinemas, or the sense of event that was created when television shows were broadcast at a particular time and there was no way of recording them. If you missed it, you missed it! Think how vividly wartime rationing and blackouts are remembered in the folklore of modern Britain. In East Germany, there is a word to describe the fond remembrance of certain aspects of the communist era; the word is *Ostalgie*, meaning "Nostalgia for the East." This takes many forms, but what is common to them seems to be a memory of social solidarity in difficult times.

Stories of travelers stranded on deserted islands have always been popular. In modern times, the popularity of survivalist shows like *I'm a Celebrity, Get Me Out of Here!*, or the various documentaries made by Bear Grylls, show that millions of us are enthralled by the spectacle of people enduring hostile conditions, or having to get by with very little.

When it comes to religion, the importance of mortification and fasting may be greatly downplayed in our era, but Lent—the period of fasting before Easter—continues to fascinate. "Are you giving up anything for Lent?" is a popular topic for conversation. Even non-practicing Christians often "give up something" for Lent—in fact, sometimes even completely non-religious people do so.

Some of the more spectacular forms of mortification also remain popular, perhaps because they are a challenge. The Lough Derg pilgrimage in Ireland is an example. Lough Derg is a lake in county Donegal, on the Northern coast of Ireland. On an island on this lake, Our Lord is said to have shown St. Patrick (5th century) a gate to purgatory. This is how its official website describes the Lough Derg pilgrimage:

> The traditional Three Day Pilgrimage follows a 1000 year old pattern. As soon as you arrive on the Island you take off your shoes and socks. You start the traditional series of Station prayers, walking around the penitential beds.
>
> At 10 pm you begin a 24-hour vigil which ends when you go to bed on the second night.
>
> You leave the Island on the morning of the third day, although your fast continues until midnight.

Hundreds of thousands of pilgrims have managed to complete this pilgrimage, thought to be the toughest in all of Europe, perhaps even in the whole Christian world.

Pilgrims are allowed one Lough Derg meal on each day of their pilgrimage, consisting of toast (without butter), oatcakes and tea/coffee (without milk). On the third day of the pilgrimage, once pilgrims have departed from the island they are permitted to take soft drinks. Still water is allowed at all times throughout the pilgrimage and drinking fountains are available, while bottled water is available to purchase in the souvenir shop.[1]

It may not sound very enticing, but every year it draws new penitents, and not all of them are believing Christians.

Tough as the Lough Derg pilgrimage is, it's baby stuff compared to some of the mortifications and penances that the saints have imposed on themselves through history. (A word regarding terminology: *penance* is an act by which we express sorrow for our sins. Mortification is aimed more at gaining control over our desires and temptations. In practice, they overlap. For the sake of convenience, I will continue to use the term "mortification" for both.) I could fill this entire book with examples of the saints' mortifications. Indeed, some of the stories of saints' mortifications are almost terrifying.

One missionary to Central America, the Franciscan priest Junipero Serra, was known to smash a large stone against his chest when preaching on the subject of repentance. On another occasion, when preaching, he began to whip himself with a chain. He suffered from a leg injury all his life because, when he landed in Mexico, he insisted on walking the distance from the coast to Mexico City. In this he was following very strictly the guidelines of St. Francis, who said that his disciples should not ride horses unless compelled to do so by necessity. Most of his fellow friars, taking a looser interpretation of their founder's guidelines, decided to ride instead.

Another saint whose mortifications are astonishing is St. Rose of

1 Lough Derg, *The Heart of Lough Derg.* http://www.loughderg.org/season-guide/three-day-pilgrimage (accessed May 27, 2017).

Lima (1586–1617), a Peruvian saint who became the first Catholic saint of the American continent, as well as the patron saint of all South America.

St. Rose of Lima

St. Rose was particularly noted for wearing a crown with iron spikes that dug into her scalp, in imitation of the crown of thorns the Roman soldiers made Jesus wear during his Crucifixion. This is how one biographer describes her austerities:

> She was deeply penetrated with a sense of her own nothingness and misery. It was to her an insupportable cross to see herself honored; her humility could not bear to hear a word of praise; and on this account hearing, one day, Michael Garrez, canon of the cathedral of Lima, who had come to visit Don Gonzalez, her intimate friend, praising her in the course of the conversation, and extolling the favours she had received from Almighty God, she retired into

her chamber, where she began to strike her breast, to weep and groan, in the presence of God; and to punish herself for giving, as she thought, a false opinion of herself to men, she gave herself several blows on the head, to force in more deeply the iron points of the crown which she always wore concealed under her veil.[2]

Not content simply to wear this crown, she would adjust its position regularly so that it pressed down on different areas of her scalp. Her self-denial was also legendary:

She was known to make a moderate sized loaf and a pitcher of water last fifty days. Another time she remained seven weeks without drinking a drop of water or any other liquor; and towards the end of her life she sometimes passed several successive days without eating or drinking. She frequently shut herself up on Thursday in her oratory, and remained there till Saturday without food or sleep, and so completely absorbed in God in a sort of ecstasy, that she continued there, immovable, and as if incapable of rising from the place where she was praying on her knees. She once passed eight entire days without any food but the bread of angels, which she received in the Holy Communion; and her supernatural abstinence was so well known to all the inhabitants of Lima, that they were aware she passed weeks without eating or drinking; and that when necessity compelled her to drink a little water to assuage the burning heat, which consumed her, she took it warm, to mortify sensuality in the pleasure she might have felt from drinking cold water.[3]

It should be pointed out that St. Rose's mortifications were not an end in themselves, but one part of a life marked by holiness and charity. She was famed for her generosity to the poor. When she died, God gave a special sign of approval to her mortifications, according to one story:

2 Rev F.W. Faber D.D., *The Life of St. Rose of Lima* (New York: P.J. Kennedy and Sons, 1855), 45–46.

3 Ibid., 56–57.

After her death a great servant of God, kissing respectfully that instrument of penance [her "crown of thorns"], felt himself interiorly inflamed with the love of God, and was at the same time perfumed with a heavenly odour, which was a sign to him that Almighty God had accepted this new sort of torture, which the blessed Rose had invented to mortify herself.[4]

Of course, a person can perform mortifications in the wrong spirit—indeed, they can be an occasion of pride and self-congratulation. St. Paul seemed to foresee this at the very dawn of Christianity when he wrote: "If I give all I possess to the poor and give over my body to hardship that I may boast, but do not have love, I gain nothing" (1 Corinthians 13:3).

Indeed, mortifications whose motives are good can also be misguided. St. Catherine Ricci (1522–1590), who was Prioress (i.e., head) of a monastery of Dominican sisters, once wrote a letter to a layman with the following advice:

Religious who are separated from the world, and who have neither business nor family obligations are bound to lead a much more mortified and rigorous life. But you as the head of a great house with all the cares of a family upon your shoulders ought to be very prudent about preserving your life and health, not for the sake of enjoying this world's pleasures but in order to support your family as you should, and give your children a true Christian training. I would remind you that we should have to give an account at the Judgement of an indiscretion as well as our self-indulgence. Now that you are at Florence, I am afraid that no-one will think of giving you broth and biscuits for supper, and therefore I am sending you a basket of chestnuts with the injunction to eat at least four every evening.[5]

---

4 Ibid., 69.
5 Felicity Leng, *Consecrated Spirits: An Anthology of Women's Writings Across the Centuries* (New York: Paulist Press, 2012), 81.

Although the most startling stories of mortification come from pre-modern saints, it is by no means the case that more recent saints have given up this practice.

By some accounts, Pope John Paul II was known to sleep on the floor, rather than in bed. He would disturb his bedclothes to make it look as though he had used them. If you think this is a minor mortification, by all means try it yourself, even for an hour! The same mortification was both practiced and recommended by St. Josemaría Escrivá. In his book *The Furrow*, which takes the form of advice to his "spiritual children," he writes:

> A young man who had just given himself more fully to God said: "What I need to do now is speak less, visit the sick and sleep on the floor." — Apply that to yourself.[6]

This was not the only form of mortification St. Josemaría practiced. He frequently employed "the discipline," a form of self-flagellation using a many-stranded whip called a scourge. He insisted that his apostolic efforts fared better the more he used the discipline. He also wore a cilice, a light metal chain with spikes which was worn around the thigh. The cilice is still worn by many members of Opus Dei today. These are examples of rather spectacular mortifications, but St. Josemaría was also dedicated to simpler forms of self-denial — such as refusing to lean against the back of his chair when he was sitting, refusing to look at anything out of curiosity, and drinking as little water as he could.

Here are two of my favorite St. Josemaría aphorisms on the subject of simple mortifications: "Don't say: 'That person gets on my nerves.' Think: 'That person sanctifies me.'" And: "Choose mortifications that don't mortify others." (What is the point of a mortification if it makes you so irritable you go around snapping at people?)

I have already mentioned Mary of the Incarnation, the French Ursuline nun who helped to found the first educational institute for girls in the New World. One of her own mortifications sounds particularly

---

6 St. Josemaría Escrivá, *The Furrow*. http://www.escrivaworks.org/book/furrow-chapter-29.htm (accessed May 27, 2017).

harsh — she would mix wormwood (a bitter herb) in her food. Eventually she was forbidden this mortification on grounds of health, but not before she had so injured her sense of taste that she could no longer tell one food from another. Anyone who regularly has to admit to gluttony in confession will be impressed by this particular mortification.

Mortification doesn't have to be about restricting physical comforts. Catholics have traditionally mortified their senses as well, especially their sense of sight. An example from St. John Berchmans, the Jesuit seminarian saint:

> It can be said that John had acquired over his look a control which was absolute. Following the rule given by St. Ignatius, he habitually held his eyes lowered. As he himself assured us, he needed to make a kind of effort to raise them. When, after his death, the Rector was having his portrait made, and the painter wished to know what had been the color of his eye, no one could tell him.
>
> Out of hatred for all curiosity, he made a sacrifice of even what he might have considered as opportunity for learning. The retinues and solemn entries of great personages and other brilliant spectacles which were so frequent in the Rome of that day, seemed to have for him no attraction. When it was proposed to him to assist at the coronation of Pope Gregory XV, elected in February 1621, he replied with a smile: "Since I came to Rome, I have seen one procession. That is more than enough."[7]

Before we smile patronizingly at such scruples, let us ask ourselves how much our own curiosity contributes to our quality of life. Intellectual curiosity is one thing, but how much celebrity news and trashy advertising and sheer gossip passes through our consciousness, and how much does it contribute to our mental and spiritual health? What about all the time spent on social media and the internet, doing nothing very substantial? The attraction towards "mindfulness" in our own era shows that the saints' "asceticism of the senses" was in

---

7 Hippolyte Delehaye, *St. John Berchmans* (New York: Benziger Brothers, 1921), 9.

fact far from ridiculous, even if Christian mindfulness has somewhat different motivations from secular mindfulness.

If you are starting to think that this all sounds very depressing, we should remember that the saints very often report *a deep joy* to be found in such acts of self-denial. St. Jean Vianney (1786–1859), who may be the most famous parish priest in history (he labored all his life in a small country parish), once wrote: "It is only the first step which costs; there is in mortification a sweetness and a consolation which, when once tasted, it is impossible again to dispense with; you must exhaust the cup to the bottom."[8]

If this sounds implausible, perhaps we can be inspired by the words of G.K. Chesterton, whose book *St. Francis of Assisi* contains a beautiful flight of eloquence on the subject of mortification and penance. Chesterton was making the argument that St. Francis (1182–1226) stepped into history at the end of a long process of collective mortification — the ancient pagan world had been so steeped in cruelty and sexual vice that *society as a whole* needed to be severely mortified, to cleanse it from the memory of such foulness. Christian Europe of the Middle Ages, he argues, felt a collective need for penance and mortification, to achieve this very end. But the world in which St. Francis appeared, Chesterton tells us, was one which had finally, after centuries, been purged of pagan uncleanness:

> To anyone who can appreciate atmospheres there is something clear and clean about the atmosphere of this crude and often harsh society [medieval Europe]. Its very lusts are clean; for they no have longer any smell of perversion. Its very cruelties are clean; they are not the luxurious cruelties of the amphitheatre. They come either of a very simple horror at blasphemy or a very simple fury at an insult. Gradually against this grey background beauty begins to appear, as something really fresh and delicate and above all surprising. Love returning is no longer what was once called platonic but what is still called chivalric love. The

8 Georgina Molyneux, *The Curé d'Ars: A Memoir of Jean-Baptiste Marie Vianney: Vol. II* (London: Saunders, Otley and Co., 1868), 243.

flowers and stars have recovered their first innocence. Fire and water are felt to be worthy to be the brother and sister of a saint. The purge of paganism is complete at last.

For water itself has been washed. Fire itself has been purified as by fire. Water is no longer the water into which slaves were flung to feed the fishes. Fire is no longer that fire through which children were passed to Moloch [a pagan god]. Flowers smell no more of the forgotten garlands gathered in the garden of Priapus [a sex god]; stars stand no more as signs of the far frigidity of gods as cold as those cold fires. They are like all new things newly made and awaiting new names, from one who shall come to name them. Neither the universe nor the earth have now any longer the old sinister significance of the world. They await a new reconciliation with man, but they are already capable of being reconciled. Man has stripped from his soul the last rag of nature worship, and can return to nature.

While it was yet twilight a figure appeared silently and suddenly on a little hill above the city, dark against the fading darkness. For it was the end of a long and stern night, a night of vigil, not unvisited by stars. He stood with his hands lifted, as in so many statues and pictures, and about him was a burst of birds singing; and behind him was the break of day.[9]

Perhaps, when we are dispirited at the prospect of any sort of penance or mortification, it would be helpful to imagine that daybreak and birdsong waiting for us on its far side.

9 G.K. Chesterton, *St. Francis of Assisi.* http://gutenberg.net.au/ebooks09/0900611.txt (accessed May 27, 2017).

Marriage

St. Louis and St. Marie Azelie Martin
Blessed Luigi Beltrame and Blessed Maria Quattrocchi
St. Elizabeth of Hungary ✳ St. Jane Frances de Chantal
St. Joaquina of Spain ✳ St. Elizabeth Ann Seton
St. Louis of France ✳ St. Margaret D'Youville
Blessed Paola Gambera-Costa

IT ALMOST GOES WITHOUT SAYING THAT THE
vast majority of saints have been unmarried, since the vast majority
of saints were drawn from the ranks of those who have taken religious
vows of celibacy—priests, religious brothers, and religious sisters.
Indeed, the Church explicitly teaches that consecrated life is a higher
calling than married life. As John Paul II wrote in *Vita Consecrata*
(1996): "As a way of showing forth the Church's holiness, it is to be
recognized that the consecrated life, which mirrors Christ's own way
of life, has an objective superiority."

Of course, this is not to say that marriage is *bad*. Indeed, Christian
tradition very often takes marital relations as a metaphor for God's
love of humanity. Take, for instance, the vision of heaven in the Book
of Revelation: "I saw the Holy City, the new Jerusalem, coming down
out of heaven from God, prepared as a bride beautifully dressed for
her husband" (Revelation 21:2).

And, although most saints are unmarried, there are quite a few
married saints. Some of them had blissfully happy marriages, while
some had miserable marriages. Some of them were married before
embarking on a life of consecrated celibacy—for instance, when their
spouses died. Some of them were ordinary married people. And some
(like Bartolo Longo, whom we have already met) were married, but
lived a life of celibacy within marriage.

Indeed, the greatest saint of all belongs to this final category. Jesus's mother, the Blessed Virgin Mary, was married, but remained a virgin all her life. The same obviously applies to St. Joseph, also one of the greatest saints of all time. (Some apocryphal writings claim that he was previously married, but there is no reason to believe this. At any rate, his marriage to the Blessed Virgin was certainly celibate.) We know from the Bible that St. Peter, the first Pope, was married at one stage of his life, as we are told that Jesus cured Peter's mother-in-law of a fever. (Centuries of jokers have wondered how St. Peter's devotion to Jesus survived this test.)

In a book entitled *Married Saints*, published in 1935, Selden Delany wrote: "It is a long time since any married saint has been officially canonized by the Catholic Church. That so few married people have been raised to the Church's altars since the present process of canonization was initiated, raises the question of whether sanctity is necessarily incompatible with married life."[1]

Well, things have changed since then. In 2015, Louis Martin and Marie Azelie Guerin, the parents of St. Thérèse of Lisieux, were canonized. Their canonization process had been rather rapid — they were pronounced venerable only in 1994. They became the first married couple to be canonized together. Given that St. Thérèse is undoubtedly the most popular saint of the modern world, it is perhaps not surprising that this popularity has extended to her parents. In the past few months, I have seen their picture in a church shrine in Dublin, and on the cover of a book dedicated to them in a Christian bookshop. As with many saints, even looking at their picture gives us a sense of their holiness. It is easy to see them as an image of our Blessed Mother and St. Joseph.

It's hard to imagine a couple more dedicated to God than Louis and Marie. Both of them sought to enter religious orders before their marriage, but were unable to do so — because of an inability to master Latin in the case of Louis, and because of health reasons in the case of Marie.

---

1 Selden Delany, *Married Saints* (Westminster: Ayer Co. Pub., 1935), 1.

Zélie Martin *St. Louis Martin*

When Marie ("Zélie") was unable to enter the religious order, she formulated this prayer for herself: "Lord, since, unlike my sister, I am not worthy to be your bride, I will enter the married state to fulfil your holy will. I beg of you to give me many children and let them be consecrated to you." She was crossing a bridge when she first saw her husband-to-be, and a voice told her: "This is he whom I have prepared for you." Nevertheless, although Zélie had discovered a vocation to married life, the desire to enter a religious order still haunted her. When she visited her sister's convent after her marriage, she "cried as she had never cried in her life."

Like Our Lady and St. Joseph, Louis and Marie decided to live a life of celibacy within marriage. They persevered in this for about a year before their priest persuaded them to consummate their union. They had nine children, four of whom died in childhood. The other five all entered religious life. Anyone who has read St. Thérèse's autobiography *Story of a Soul* is charmed by its glimpse into a pious Christian home overflowing with affection (though Zélie died early in St. Thérèse's life). Interestingly, considering that saints Louis and Marie lost four children at a young age, both of the miracles approved as part of their canonization process involved the healing of newborn babies. Zélie took to motherhood; once, hearing that a woman in the neighborhood had given birth to triplets, she cried out: "What a happy mother! If I only had twins! But I shall never know that joy!"

Both of these saintly spouses rose at five a.m., and attended 5:30 Mass every morning. Louis was particularly austere; he did not smoke or drink alcohol, sit with his legs crossed, eat between meals, or sit beside the fire unless he really needed to. He was known for his spontaneous charity; once, he handed his hat around at a train station to raise funds for a homeless epileptic, adding a substantial donation himself. The collection was enough for the epileptic to afford medical treatment, for the first time ever. On another occasion, Louis brought a drunken workman, who was lying down in the street, home to his house, giving him a stern lecture in the morning.

His wife could also be stern when it was necessary. Although her daughters remember her sweetness, there were occasions when she put her foot down. Once, when a maid dressed her daughter Céline as a boy as a part of some game, Zélie — who considered this immodest — stopped the game and gave the maid a dressing-down. On another occasion, she noticed a friend who had been playing with her daughters calling one of them into the garden for a secretive talk. She reproached this friend, sent her home, and warned her daughters to be on the lookout for bad influences. Both these examples of discipline might be considered "repressive" today — yet it was this mother who raised a saint, and other holy children.

There is something especially inspiring in the thought of a saintly married couple. Jokes, fiction and casual conversation tend to paint marriage as a "ball and chain," even if it is seen as a highly desirable ball and chain. The *best* that can be hoped for in marriage is that the man and woman will get along most of the time — or so we might think, from how it is spoken about. The husband and wife's priorities and interests are assumed to clash — the stereotype is of the husband ignoring his wife while he watches football (or plays computer games), or of the wife forcing her husband to stand for hours in a clothes shop, bored out of his mind. In our age of feminism, and some of the ugly reactions against feminism on the male side, the idea that *the sexes really are complementary* is often difficult to believe. We might accept the saintly marriage of St. Joseph and the Blessed Virgin, if we are Catholics — but then, they had a special mission from God, and presumably they were given all the grace needed to fulfill it. But when we read about a saintly married couple from the nineteenth century, it reassures us that husbands and wives really *can* be companions, and fellow pilgrims on the quest for holiness.

As well as this, the picture of a saintly family (as the Martins were saintly) shows that sanctity is not a freak, a mere flash in the pan. It is not the case that a saint would be impossible to live with, or would not fit in with domestic life. If a household of saints can exist, so could a society of saints, despite the frequent claim that, if Christianity were actually *followed*, society would fall apart. (This is how the Irish writer Anthony Cronin put it: "The truth is that Jesus Christ was a classical anarchist and, whether or not he desired an immediate transformation of society along anarchist lines, he enjoined the kind of anarchism on his followers which, if they were sufficiently numerous, would bring it about.")[2] The beatitudes of Jesus — turning the other cheek, going the extra mile, and so forth — are (such critics suggest) so radical that they would make society untenable in its current form. A household is a society in miniature; and the household of the St. Thérèse's family seems to have worked perfectly well.

For parents raising children, or those who hope to be parents one day, Zélie's approach to teaching her children religion may be of interest. Instead of burdening their minds with abstract theological concepts, she told them to pray and to make sacrifices for particular purposes — for instance, to get a deceased relative out of purgatory sooner. She urged them to do good deeds as "pearls in their crowns," leading them to think of heavenly things rather than earthly things from the very start.

---

2 Anthony Cronin, *An Irish Eye* (Dingle: Brandon Book Publishers, 1985), 73.

Louis and Zélie were not the first couple to be beatified. That distinction must go to Luigi Beltrame Quattrocchi (died 1951) and his wife Maria (died 1965), who were beatified by St. John Paul II in 2001. They were an Italian couple who were organizers in many Catholic organizations, and who were also members of the Third Order of St. Francis (a lay division of the Franciscans). Like St. Gianna Beretta Molla (died 1962), another married saint who famously sacrificed her life so that her unborn child might live, Maria went ahead with a difficult pregnancy which might have resulted in her own death. Indeed, she was told she had only a five per cent chance of living if she went ahead with the birth. However, both mother and child survived it in full health. The Quattrocchi household was consecrated to the Sacred Heart of Jesus and recited a family rosary every day. While the parents of St. Thérèse lived a celibate marriage at the beginning, and only consummated it later, Maria and Luigi had quite the opposite path; they embraced celibacy after twenty years of marriage, in a bid to draw closer to God.

When it comes to happily married saints, the story of St. Elizabeth of Hungary (1207–1231) is particularly charming. She was the daughter of the King of Hungary, and was married in an arranged marriage to Ludwig, Count of Thuringia and Hesse (in central Germany). Though the marriage was an arranged one, it was full of love. This is how one writer describes it:

> Elizabeth's love for her husband was the natural fruit of the pure friendship which began in their childhood. Even after their marriage, they addressed each other as "dear brother" and "dear sister." It was not, however, what one might call a purely spiritual love. Those who regard that sort of love as a necessary adjunct of sanctity should read an account of their married life. They were passionately devoted to each other. No romance could be more touching. She could scarcely bear being parted from him when he went on a journey or on a military expedition; to serve the Emperor or to make a visit to Rome. To quote from Ida Condenhove's study of the Saint:

"Then she cannot be parted from him, follows him for days in all weathers; puts on widow's weeds. So passionately does she cling to the sight of the beloved, so much does she hunger for him, so deeply even to the heart's core does she know, does she feel, the bliss of remaining for work or rest, in the warm, living presence of a beloved being. And boundless is the passion of her joy, her starved longing for his tenderness, when he returns — impetuously, heedless of his retinue she throws herself into his arms and cannot let go of him, so insatiable is her joy at the sight of him."[3]

Indeed, it is said that St. Elisabeth's affection for her husband could be excessive:

According to some of her medieval biographers, the possibility that her passionate love for her husband might make her forget God was impressed upon her mind one day at Mass. She found herself gazing admiringly at her husband, who was attired in festal array. She forgot where she was, until the bell rang for the consecration. She glanced at the altar just as the priest was elevating the host, and perceived that it was bleeding! Overwhelmed with remorse, she lingered long in the Church weeping and disconsolate over the sign that had been given her.[4]

Even during her marriage, St. Elisabeth devoted herself to charitable works. Once she was found cutting and washing the hair of a man who had a disease of the scalp. After her husband died in the Crusades, she founded a hospital and served the poor in it, wearing the habit of a Franciscan tertiary. She died at the age of twenty-four.

What is appealing about *this* picture of a happy marriage is the affection to be found within it. St. Elisabeth, it would seem, was "silly" about her husband. Saints may sometimes seem inhuman in their ferocious charity towards humanity in general. It is reassuring to know

---

3 Selden Delany, *Married Saints* (Westminster: Ayer Co. Pub., 1935), 95–96.
4 Ibid., 96–97.

that they can also feel enormous affection towards particular people.

Another instance of a saint's happy marriage is that of St. Jeanne de Chantal (1572–1641), foundress of the Congregation of the Visitation, an order of enclosed religious women. As Ronda de Sola Chervin, author of *Treasury of Women Saints*, writes: "At twenty she married the Baron de Chantal and had a very happy marriage. They had four children. After just eight years of marriage, Jeanne's beloved husband was killed in a hunting accident. The interior experiences Jeanne had at that time was to color her future. Her inordinate, prostrating grief of four month's duration led her to realize the passing nature of things and to attach herself all the more intensely to the Lord Jesus."[5]

Just like St. Marie of the Sacred Heart, St. Jane Frances de Chantal faced opposition from her teenage son when she entered religious life. Indeed, she literally had to step over his body as she left her home for the last time, as he prostrated himself in front of her. If you think that is harsh, perhaps we should remember the words of Our Lord: "Anyone who loves their father or mother more than me is not worthy of me; anyone who loves their son or daughter more than me is not worthy of me" (Matthew 10:37).

There are many other examples of saints who lived happy married lives before entering religious life. St. Joaquina of Spain (1783–1854), future foundress of the Carmelite Sisters of Charity, yearned to be a nun even when she was a little girl. However, her parents arranged a marriage for her with a lawyer of noble birth named Teodoro. After they were married, Teodoro revealed to her that he, too, had wished to enter religious life. However, they embraced the marital state, and had nine children together before Teodoro died. Their marriage was a pious and contented one; they attended Mass and said the rosary together every day.

The first saint to be born in the United States of America, Elizabeth Ann Seton (1774–1821), was happily married to a partner in a merchant shipping business. They had five children, but she was left a widow at the age of twenty-nine. At this time she was an Episcopalian, but after

---

5 Ronda de Sola Chervin, *Treasury of Woman Saints* (Cork: The Mercier Press, 1991), 77.

a trip to Italy, she began to be drawn to the Catholic faith. When she finally converted, she faced bitter hostility from former friends. She went on to form the American Sisters of Charity.

So far, aside from our saintly couples, we have looked at the marriages of female saints. A male saint who enjoyed a happy marriage was St. Louis of France (1214–1270). St. Louis must have been one of the most blessed men in history; as well as becoming a saint and having a happy marriage, he was king of France. His death, though heroic, was less happy (at least from a worldly perspective); he died of dysentery in Tunisia, on the Eighth Crusade.

King Louis's marriage was an arranged one; his mother found him a wife in Margaret of Provence, a woman of notable piety. Despite having arranged the marriage herself, the saint's mother grew jealous of Margaret, on account of King Louis's devotion to her. They had eleven children. It was not always an easy marriage—at one point, King Louis asked the Pope to nullify an oath his queen had persuaded their son to make, a vow of obedience to his mother until the age of thirty—but it was marked by a courtesy and deference which might be thought surprising for its time. When the King was captured, his queen became the only woman to lead a crusade when she negotiated for his release. We can see St. Louis's courtesy in the following passage, again from Selden Delany:

> Throughout their married life, Louis never entered upon any serious undertaking without first gaining the permission of his wife. Father R.P. Surin, of the Society of Jesus, writing in 1652, praises this habit of the French king as exemplifying the quality of wisdom in conjugal love: "It is reported of St. Louis that he never disposed of his person without taking the advice of Madame Marguerite of Provence, his wife; and that when in captivity in the Holy Land, when he was treating of his ransom, before giving his final word, he demanded the privilege of speaking to the queen, who had accompanied him in the voyage of the Levant. Upon the infidels expressing their surprise, he replied that he could conclude nothing without her, *because she was his Lady,*

and as such he owed her this respect. To act and speak in that way proved the wise love of the holy king for the queen his wife."[6]

Of course, not all married saints have had happy marriages. Another foundress of a religious order, the Canadian St. Margaret D'Youville (1701–1771), had a disastrous marriage. (She was educated at a school founded by St. Marie of the Incarnation, about whom we have read already.) This marriage is described by her biographer, Mother Mary G. Dufin:

> Among the many suitors who disputed her hand, Marguerite favored Mr. Francois Madeleine D'Youville, a handsome, fascinating gentleman from Montreal. Their courtship was short…. She soon found that her husband was minus all the qualities necessary to ensure a livelihood for her children and to make a home for a family. He was extravagant, vain and spent his fortune in gambling and dissipation. He became hard and cruel and abandoned his sweet young wife to loneliness and the vexations of an irritable, jealous mother-in-law. Though anguish and fear for the future of her little ones filled Marguerite's soul, still her mother's heart found comfort in the caresses of the five little darlings God had set her. The clouds hung heavy and black over her lonely home, but soon a ray of divine light pierced the darkness, revealing to her generous soul the boundless love of the Eternal Father for his earthly children and the inexhaustible treasures His Providence has in store for those who trust Him alone…. Eight years of married life had elapsed when her husband, still in the prime of his thirty years, was suddenly stricken, and after a few days' illness succumbed on July 4, 1730. It was at this trying moment that Madame D'Youville gave proof of her wonderful virtue. Far from rejoicing that the cross was lifted from her weary shoulders, she sincerely grieved for the husband to whom she had vowed her love and fidelity but who, alas, had proved himself so unworthy. [7]

6 Selden Delany, *Married Saints* (Westminster: Ayer Co. Pub., 1935), 113.
7 Mother Mary G. Duffin, *A Heroine of Charity: Venerable Mother d'Youville: Foundress*

When St. Marie was widowed in 1730, she had to open a shop to support her two sons — she had lost four other children in infancy. Despite all this, she soldiered on, and God reaped an abundant harvest from her adversities; both of her sons eventually became priests, and she herself went on to found the order of the Grey Nuns, whose various offshoots now operate in four countries, operating hospitals, women's shelters, and other institutions.

The married life of Blessed Paola Gambera-Costa (1473–1515) is a combination of suffering and redemption. This Italian noblewoman longed to be a nun, but her parents arranged a marriage to a nobleman who lived a lavish lifestyle. He later acquired a mistress, even inviting her to live in their castle with them. He ridiculed Paola for her charitable works, which led the couples' servants to ridicule her as well. Paola — who had joined the Third Order of St. Francis — showed her forgiveness by nursing her husband's mistress when she fell ill and died. This led to her husband's conversion, and for the last four years of his life the couple lived in harmony. Early in her marriage, Blessed Paola vowed never to criticize her husband, and she kept to her vow through all their difficulties.

Marriage for the saints, then, seems to have been not so different from marriage for the rest of us — joyous for some, tragic for others, a mixed bag for yet others. Perhaps this chapter will inspire married people to believe that they, too, can seek sanctity — whether their marriage is happy, unhappy, or a combination of the two.

of the Sisters of Charity Grey Nuns, Montreal, 1701–1777 (New York: Benziger Brothers, 1938), 34–36.

Family

St. Pappin of Ballymun
St. Benedict and St. Scholastica ✳ St. Francis of Assisi
St. Thomas Aquinas ✳ St. Rose of Lima
St. Germaine de Pibrac ✳ Blessed Laura Vicuña
St. Thomas More

YOU THINK YOUR FAMILY IS BAD? WAIT TILL YOU
hear about the saints' families!

Actually, the experience of the saints with their families is very
similar to the experience of the saints with marriage — good, bad and
everything in between. However, there does seem to be a surprising
number of cases in which saints have faced strong hostility and opposition from their own families. But perhaps this is not so surprising,
after all. The Holy Spirit often calls saints to take radical steps, steps
which are (sometimes understandably) opposed by their parents,
spouses, siblings, children and other relatives. Saints do extraordinary
things, and this can often appear to be attention-seeking, or even a
symptom of mental illness. The goodness of a saint can make others
all-too-conscious of their sins and imperfections — something which
often leads to jealousy and resentment. And (although it is not fashionable to mention this) we must take into account that Satan and
his demons are always working to take advantage of family tensions
and conflicts.

Jesus himself warned his followers that his demands might cause
domestic upheaval: "Do not suppose that I have come to bring peace
to the earth. I did not come to bring peace, but a sword. For I have
come to turn a man against his father, a daughter against her mother,
a daughter-in-law against her mother-in-law. A man's enemies will be
the members of his own household. Anyone who loves their father or

mother more than me is not worthy of me; anyone who loves their son or daughter more than me is not worthy of me" (Matthew 10:34–37).

Thankfully, hostility has not been the universal experience of saints with their families: we have already seen several examples of the opposite. Perhaps St. Thérèse of Lisieux is the most remarkable: a saint born to a husband and wife who were themselves saints. The local saint of Ballymun, the Dublin suburb where I grew up, provides another (if considerably less well-known!) example. St. Pappin was the son of a provincial king who died in the sixth century. The fact that he was a king's son might not be as remarkable as it sounds; there were many small kingdoms in Ireland at this time. What *is* remarkable, however, is that St. Pappin's four brothers — Colman, Folloman, Jernoe and Naal — were all saints, too!

Perhaps the most famous sibling saints (outside the two pairs of brothers amongst the Apostles: James and John, and Andrew and Peter) are the sixth-century saints St. Benedict of Nursa and his sister St. Scholastica, who were actually twins. St. Benedict founded the Benedictine Order and its famous monastery at Monte Cassino, and is considered the father of Western monasticism. St. Scholastica was a contemplative saint who, it is believed, founded the first female Benedictine monastery. Once a year, the brother and sister would confer on spiritual matters. The story goes that, at their last meeting, St. Scholastica asked God to create a storm so that her brother would be delayed another night in returning to his monastery. God obliged, and Scholastica died shortly afterwards.

We have already seen how it was a brother and sister (Jacinta and Francisco) and their cousin Lucia to whom our Blessed Mother revealed herself in the Fatima apparitions. All three children were devoted to one another. Sadly, not all saints have had such a happy experience of family.

Though I have described St. Thérèse as the most popular saint of modern times, St. Francis of Assisi (died 1226) must be a close contender. Indeed, reading the lives of the saints, I have sometimes wondered if St. Francis is unfairly elevated over others. Though he founded the Franciscan Order and invented the Christmas crib, there are any number of less celebrated saints whose feats of charity and renunciation have been no less spectacular. This is particularly galling when critics of Christianity cite St. Francis as an almost unique example of a Christian who followed the example of our Lord; there are plenty of others — if they would only look!

St. Francis's relations with his father were not the easiest. When the young saint had a vision of Christ, who told him to "rebuild his church," St. Francis set about rebuilding the dilapidated church in which he was praying at the time, which was called St. Damiano of Assisi. Unfortunately, in order to do so, he took his father's financial assistance for granted. As G.K. Chesterton wrote, in his biography of the saint:

> Francis sprang up and went. To go and do something was one of the driving demands of his nature; probably he had gone and done it before he had at all thoroughly thought out what he had done. In any case what he had done was something very decisive and immediately very disastrous for his singular social career. In the coarse conventional language of the uncomprehending world, he stole. From his own enthusiastic point of view, he extended to his venerable father Peter Bernadone the exquisite excitement and inestimable privilege of assisting, more or less unconsciously, in the rebuilding of St. Damien's Church. In point of fact what he did first was to sell his own horse and then go off and sell several bales of his father's cloth, making the sign of the cross over them to indicate their pious and charitable destination. Peter Bernadone did not see things in this light. Peter Bernadone indeed had not very much light to see by, so far as understanding the genius and temperament of his extraordinary son was concerned.[1]

The event led to a protracted dispute between father and son, which involved Francis's father imprisoning the saint. The matter was eventually brought before a bishop, who demanded Francis return the money to his father:

---

1 G.K. Chesterton, *St. Francis of Assisi*. http://gutenberg.net.au/ebooks09/0900611.txt (accessed May 28, 2017).

He stood up before them all and said, "Up to this time I have
called Pietro Bernadone father, but now I am the servant of
God. Not only the money but everything that can be called his
I will restore to my father, even the very clothes he has given
me." And he rent off all his garments except one; and they saw
that it was a hair-shirt.

He piled the garments in a heap on the floor and threw the
money on top of them. Then he turned to the bishop, and received
his blessing, like one who turns his back on society; and, according
to the account, went out as he was into the cold world. Apparently it was literally a cold world at the moment, and snow was
on the ground.[2]

In this instance, it's hard not to have sympathy with the saint's put-
upon father. It is doubtless not always easy to be a saint's relative. Sadly,
there is no reason to believe they were ever reconciled.

The writer whose biography of St. Francis I have been quoting, G.K.
Chesterton (1874–1936), is himself being investigated as a possible
saint. (I write more about him in an appendix at the back of the book.)
Chesterton's other biography of a saint, *St. Thomas Aquinas: The Dumb
Ox*, chronicles another conflict between a major saint and his family.

St. Thomas Aquinas (1225–1274) was, along with St. Augustine of
Hippo, one of the two greatest thinkers in the history of Christianity.
The intellectual system he created, which draws on many previous
thinkers (pagan, Christian and even Islamic) is called Thomism. There
are whole academic journals and conferences devoted to his thought,
and several popes have emphasized the continual importance of his
writings to the defense of Catholic teaching.

St. Thomas, the son of a noble family (like many saints in the history
of the Church) was determined to join the Dominican Order — at the
time, a new order who, with their involvement in religious controversy
and their begging for alms, seemed less respectable than the established
orders. His family had no objection to his entering religious life, but

2 Ibid.

they had earmarked him for a high position in the Benedictine Order. As Chesterton wrote:

> It would seem that the young Thomas Aquinas walked into his father's castle one day and calmly announced that he had become one of the Begging Friars, of the new order founded by Dominic the Spaniard; much as the eldest son of the squire might go home and airily inform the family that he had married a gypsy; or the heir of a Tory Duke state that he was walking tomorrow with the Hunger Marchers organised by alleged Communists. By this, as has been noted already, we may pretty well measure the abyss between the old monasticism and the new, and the earthquake of the Dominican and Franciscan revolution. Thomas had appeared to wish to be a Monk; and the gates were silently opened to him and the long avenues of the abbey, the very carpet, so to speak, laid for him up to the throne of the mitred abbot. He said he wished to be a Friar, and his family flew at him like wild beasts; his brothers pursued him along the public roads, half-rent his friar's frock from his back and finally locked him up in a tower like a lunatic.[3]

His family not only held him captive in a castle, but at one point tried to break his dedication to a life of chastity by sending a prostitute to his room:

> His brothers introduced into his room some specially gorgeous and painted courtesan, with the idea of surprising him by a sudden temptation, or at least involving him in a scandal. His anger was justified, even by less strict moral standards than his own; for the meanness was even worse than the foulness of the expedient. Even on the lowest grounds, he knew his brothers knew, and they knew that he knew, that it was an insult to him as a gentleman to suppose that he would break his pledge upon so base a provocation; and he had behind him a far more terrible

---

3 G.K. Chesterton, *St. Thomas Aquinas: The Dumb Ox*. http://gutenberg.net.au/ebooks01/0100331.txt (accessed May 28, 2017).

sensibility; all that huge ambition of humility which was to him the voice of God out of heaven. In this one flash alone we see that huge unwieldy figure in an attitude of activity, or even animation; and he was very animated indeed. He sprang from his seat and snatched a brand out of the fire, and stood brandishing it like a flaming sword. The woman not unnaturally shrieked and fled, which was all that he wanted; but it is quaint to think of what she must have thought of that madman of monstrous stature juggling with flames and apparently threatening to burn down the house. All he did, however, was to stride after her to the door and bang and bar it behind her; and then, with a sort of impulse of violent ritual, he rammed the burning brand into the door, blackening and blistering it with one big black sign of the cross.[4]

Eventually, giving up the captivity as a lost cause, his family discreetly let him "escape" from the castle, and St. Thomas commenced a glittering career as a theological and philosophical writer — and a member of the Dominican Order.

We have already touched on the life of St. Rose of Lima, the patron saint of South America, famous for wearing a crown of thorns with iron spikes, and other ferocious mortifications. One mortification that St. Rose had to endure, and which was not of her own choosing, was the opposition of her family:

Her mother found fault with everything she did; she condemned her reserve, she blamed her fasts, she did not like her taking up so much time in prayer, nor her retired life, so opposite to the maxims of the world; for these reasons, she often scolded her, and went so far as to use a thousand abusive epithets as if she had been an infamous person. At the least provocation she gave her blows on the cheek; but when she was carried away by anger, she put no bounds to her ill-usage; she was not content with abusing her, striking her on the face, and kicking her; she

4 Ibid.

took a thick knotty stick and struck her with all her strength. She began to treat her thus when she cut off her hair after having consecrated her virginity to God, and she continued the same treatment on many occasions.

Those with whom she lived were actuated towards her by so extraordinary a spirit of envy and vexation, because they saw her lead a life so different from theirs, that they did everything they could to disoblige her; they even threatened to report her to the Inquisition as a deluded girl and a hypocrite, who deceived the world by a false appearance of virtue.[5]

Stepmothers have an unfair reputation, especially in fairy tales. But real-life wicked stepmothers exist too. St. Germaine de Pibrac (1579–1601) had to endure such a cross. This French saint, born to a farming family, lost her mother when she was still an infant, and also developed scrofula — a disfiguring skin disease. She also had a withered hand from birth, which made her less useful for farm work. When her father remarried, his new wife treated St. Germaine abominably, beating her and mocking her. She would not let Germaine stay in the house, saying that she was in danger of infecting the other children of the family with scrofula. She had to sleep in the stable, or on a bed of twisted vines.

St. Germaine lived a holy life in spite of all this persecution. She shared her food with the poor, gave religious instruction to local children, and prayed the rosary on a piece of knotted string. She had trained her sheep so well that they would not wander off when she went to Mass. The cruel stepmother's attitude was changed by a miracle. One winter's day, she accused St. Germaine of stealing bread and hiding it in her apron, and she was about to beat her with a stick. St. Germaine opened the folds of her apron, and summer flowers fell out. This miracle changed the attitude of her stepmother, and the saint was invited to live in the house again. However, she chose to remain living as she had.

St. Germaine died at the age of twenty-two, and was buried in the local church. During a renovation of the church forty years later, her

---

5   Rev F.W. Faber D.D., *The Life of St. Rose of Lima* (New York: P.J. Kennedy and Sons, 1855), 122–123.

body was found to be incorrupt; that is, it had not decayed. Hundreds of miracles were attributed to her intercession.

This saint's experience is inspiring because so many of us are trapped in difficult situations — whether it's a family situation, a health situation, or some other situation. We might be tempted to think that we would pursue lives of holiness if only we could get out of our current mess. However, it might well be that "our current mess" is the very means of sanctification that God has given us.

Blessed Laura Vicuña

Very few saints have had a worse family situation than that of Blessed Laura Vicuña (1891–1904). This Chilean girl offered her own life to save her mother from an immoral relationship. She lost her father at the age of three, which put the burden on her mother to support Laura and her sister. While traveling in search of work, the unfortunate woman met Manuel Mora, a ranch-owner who offered to pay for the girls' education, and to protect the family. However, the condition was that Laura's mother would become Manuel's lover.

Laura attended a school run by religious sisters, and developed into a pious and intelligent girl. However, she had to endure advances from her mother's lover at an early age. When she was only eleven, she asked a priest, during confession, to be allowed to offer her life for the conversion of her mother from her immoral way of life. The priest, impressed by her seriousness, allowed her to make this offer to God.

When Manuel Mora's advances towards her daughter became more persistent, Laura's mother fled from his ranch, bringing the two girls with her. Her lover followed them into their new abode, brandishing a whip and demanding they return with him. When Laura left the house, Manuel followed her into the street, whipped her, and tried to mount her on his horse to carry her back with him. When some locals came to intervene, he abandoned the girl in the street. A week later she died. Before she died, she said to her mother: "Mama, I'm dying, but I'm happy to offer my life for you. I asked Our Lord for this." Before Laura expired, her mother promised her she would return to the practice of the Faith. She lived up to the promise, making her confession shortly after her daughter's death.

After such a somber tale, perhaps it is best to close this chapter with a picture of a happy family life. St. Thomas More was executed in 1535 by King Henry VIII for refusing to acknowledge him (rather than the Pope) as the head of the English Church. St. Thomas had been Lord Chancellor, the highest position in the English legal system. More had been married twice, his first wife having died after bearing him four children. He adopted the daughter of his second wife, a woman who was seven years older than himself. More was a man of tremendous learning and culture, and his biographer Christopher Hollis draws a charming picture of his homestead:

> He may be almost called the patron saint of family life. Of his life there we have so many and such vivid pictures and his happiness came to him so largely from it. His happiness was thus a happiness that does not differ in kind from that that is offered to every normal man and woman…. [Hollis goes on to quote a letter from St. Thomas's friend Erasmus:] "[His wife is] an active and vigilant housewife with whom he lives as pleasantly and sweetly as if she had all the charms of youth. You will scarcely find a husband who by authority or severity has gained such ready compliance as More by playful flattery. What indeed would he not obtain when he has prevailed on a woman already getting

old, by no means of a pliable disposition and intent on domestic affairs, to play the harp, the lute, the monochord and the flute and by the appointment of her husband to devote to this task a fixed time every day? With the same address [i.e., in the same way] he guides his whole household in which there are no disturbances or strife. If such arise he immediately appeases it and sets all right again, never conceiving enmity himself nor making an enemy. Indeed there seems to be a kind of fateful happiness in this house so that no one has lived in it without rising to higher fortune; no member of it has ever incurred any stain on his reputation. You will scarcely find any who live in such harmony with a mother as does Thomas More with his step-mother, for his father had married again and the son was affectionate towards her as to his own mother. Quite recently he has married a third wife and More swears he never knew a better woman. Towards his parents and his sisters his love is never intrusive or exacting while he omits nothing that can show his sincere attachment…. More has been careful to have all his children from their earliest years thoroughly imbued first with chaste and holy morals, and then with polite letters. His wife, who excels in good sense and experience rather than learning, governs the little company with wonderful tact, assigning to each a task and requiring its performance, allowing no one to be idle or occupied in trifles."[6]

St. Thomas More eventually had to leave this domestic idyll for an appointment with the executioner—and to win a martyr's crown. But while it lasted, it was a demonstration that saints are not obligated to renounce the "respectable" virtues, or ordinary life, or simple happiness when it is available. There is nothing banal, insipid, or "chocolate box" about a happy home. The idea that Christianity *always* has to be counter-cultural, in every respect, is a fallacy.

As with marriage, the family lives of the saints teach us that every family situation can be a path to sanctity.

6 Christopher Hollis, *Thomas More* (Milwaukee: The Bruce Publishing Company, 1934), 37–44.

Chastity

Blessed John Henry Newman ✳ St. Aloysius Gonzaga
St. Elizabeth of the Trinity ✳ St. Alphonsa of India
St. María de las Maravillas Pidal Chico de Guzmán
St. Maria Goretti ✳ Blessed Antonia Messina
St. Charles Lwanga ✳ St. Bernard of Clairvaux
St. Frances Xavier Cabrini ✳ St. Padre Pio
Blessed Pier Giorgio Frassati

MORTIFICATION ISN'T THE ONLY CHRISTIAN VALUE which is uncongenial to the modern world. Chastity, too, is a virtue that our contemporary society tends to view with bafflement and distrust. On television and radio debates, we frequently hear the argument that Catholic priests should be allowed to marry, as the denial of their sexual desires is deeply unnatural, and must lead to all kinds of complexes and neuroses. The tragedy of sex abuse scandals involving priests, which have rocked the Catholic Church in so many countries in the last thirty years or so, is often taken as evidence that this must be the case.

The fact that the vast majority of priests do not abuse children is rarely considered as counter-evidence to this claim. The assumption seems to be that even priests who abide by their vows of celibacy are living stunted, suffocated lives. Most people who actually know priests will find it hard to take this idea seriously, since they are often more fulfilled and cheerful than people with busy "love lives."

Of course, chastity is not just about celibacy or virginity. All Christians are called to lead lives of chastity, including married people. This is how the *Catechism of the Catholic Church* defines chastity: "Chastity means the successful integration of sexuality within the person and thus the inner unity of man in his bodily and spiritual being. Sexuality, in which man's belonging to the bodily and biological world is expressed, becomes personal and truly human when it is integrated into the relationship of one person to another, in the complete and lifelong mutual gift of a man and a woman."[1]

The writer of a blog called *Why I Left Christianity* (whose tagline is: "My journey from a god-loving, baptized, good christian girl to an atheist, bisexual feminist") had this to say about the Christian attitude to sex:

> I have never understood the obsession that Christians had/have with sex (well, really the fear of it). I mean, if you use their reasoning, (which I don't, but let's try it for a minute) god made humans in his image. God is perfect and does not make mistakes. So, the way we are is the way "god" made us, right? Okay. So, god created us needing sex. All humans crave sex when they hit puberty (at least most) and I think it is pretty natural for humans to want to fulfil their cravings for sex as much as they need to eat, sleep, and drink water. Right? So why do Christians have so many hang-ups with sex? It seems that sex, homosexuality, premarital sex etc. …are on their list of "serious sins."[2]

The reader may expect me to pour cold water on this analysis. While I strongly disagree with it, I can certainly understand the writer's perspective. I think most of us can. Catholic teaching on sex is challenging for most people who live in today's society. Many of us find it hard to understand why God would create human beings with romantic and sexual desires and then encourage them to suppress those desires. Movies, TV, and literature often present romance and sex as being essential ingredients to a fulfilled life. It seems so obvious that men and women are complementary, are *meant* for each other, that in the best possible world nobody would forego the experience of love and sex.

---

1 Catholic Church, *The Catechism of the Catholic Church*. http://www.vatican.va/archive/ENG0015/_INDEX.HTM (accessed May 28, 2017).

2 Random Atheist in the Deep South, *Why I Left Christianity*. http://whyileftchristianity.blogspot.ie/2010_11_01_archive.html (accessed May 28, 2017).

And yet...there is another meaning to the word "romance," one that has nothing to do with sex, or with the relations between men and women. I once heard a priest explain that romance was what drew him to the priesthood. There is something very *romantic* about dedicating yourself to Christ so utterly that you sacrifice certain other good things, including sex. Besides this, most of us feel that our contemporary attitude to sex is not so healthy, either. Sex is used to sell movies, books, and even inanimate products in a way that it never was when our society was more Christian — at least, it had never been so blatant and unrestrained. Pornography addiction is becoming endemic, especially since the advent of the internet — not only amongst men, but increasingly amongst women, too. The fact that, within living memory, the American code of movie censorship strictly regulated the duration of onscreen kisses makes us laugh today. But who doesn't feel a certain relief in watching old movies from the era before sexual liberation — an appreciation of their gentleness, their innocence, compared to the explicitness of so much entertainment today?

Now, it's true that there is a big difference between prudishness and chastity. But sometimes one cannot help feeling the world could do with more prudishness, if prudishness means a reluctance to treat sex in a salacious or loose manner.

Besides this, we cannot help but notice that people treat the Catholic priesthood, and the consecrated life of religious sisters and brothers, as something very special. If there is a priest in a movie (especially a horror movie!), it is almost certainly going to be a Catholic priest. Anglican vicars rarely battle the forces of the demonic, at least in Hollywood. Now, I'm not suggesting this is entirely to do with celibacy; but celibacy surely has something to do with it. Celibacy is a demonstration that priests, and members of religious orders, are living a life set apart, a special vocation.

Surely we must come to the conclusion; sex is *not* something simple and straightforward. There is something about this side of our humanity which seems to *go wrong* more easily and more drastically than many other sides of our humanity. It requires especially strong safeguards to keep from running wild; and there seems to be something very special indeed about people who renounce sex and romantic love in their own lives, for the sake of a higher ideal.

I have quoted the English Catholic writer G.K. Chesterton several times now. His essay "A Piece of Chalk" expresses most eloquently the view of chastity and virginity that, even in our hyper-sexualized era, makes us regard priests and nuns with a certain deference:

> Virtue is not the absence of vices or the avoidance of moral dangers; virtue is a vivid and separate thing, like pain or a particular smell. Mercy does not mean not being cruel, or sparing people revenge or punishment; it means a plain and positive thing like the sun, which one has either seen or not seen.
>
> Chastity does not mean abstention from sexual wrong; it means something flaming, like Joan of Arc. In a word, God paints in many colours; but he never paints so gorgeously, I had almost said so gaudily, as when He paints in white.[3]

I would argue that, in our day, reading the lives of the saints is the best route to an understanding, and an appreciation, of the virtue of chastity. *Purity* may perhaps be the word that expresses this virtue. It has all the beauty of a gleaming snowfall, or the light of early morning. We know it when we see it — or even when we read about it. It speaks to our heart faster than it speaks to our head.

Amongst Christian denominations, lifelong virginity seems almost a Catholic monopoly. But it hasn't always been this way. While he was still an Anglican, Blessed John Henry Newman (1801–1890) made a vow of lifelong celibacy, as he recounts in his memoir, *Apologia Pro Vita Sua*:

> I am obliged to mention, though I do it with great reluctance, another deep imagination, which at this time, the autumn of 1816, took possession of me — there can be no mistake about the fact; — viz. that it was the will of God that I should lead a single life. This anticipation, which has held its ground almost continuously

---

3 G.K. Chesterton, "A Piece of Chalk," American Chesterton Society website. https://www.chesterton.org/a-piece-of-chalk/ (accessed May 28, 2017).

ever since—with the break of a month now and a month then, up to 1829, and, after that date, without any break at all—was more or less connected, in my mind, with the notion that my calling in life would require such a sacrifice as celibacy involved; as, for instance, missionary work among the heathen, to which I had a great drawing for some years. It also strengthened my feeling of separation from the visible world, of which I have spoken above.[4]

Blessed John Henry Newman

Newman, of course, would eventually convert to Catholicism. ("Separation from the visible world" is a good term for the kind of *specialness* that we find, even in our own day, in the Catholic priesthood.)

4 John Henry Newman, *Apologia Pro Vita Sua*. http://www.newmanreader.org/works/apologia65/chapter1.html (accessed May 28, 2017).

When we look at the lives of Catholic saints through history, we find any number of saints who made private vows of virginity at a young age. We have already considered the case of St. Aloysius Gonzaga (died 1591), who was so dedicated to chastity that he avoided even looking at women. He took a private vow of virginity when he was only nine years of age. The recently canonized St. Elizabeth of the Trinity (died 1906) took a private vow of virginity at the age of fourteen, despite describing herself as "coquettish," and despite being much sought after by suitors.

St. Alphonsa of India (1910–1946) was the daughter of a doctor, whose family belonged to the Syrio-Malabar Church. A brief note on the Syrio-Malabar Church: it is one of twenty-three "Eastern churches" within the auspices of the worldwide Catholic Church. They have their own distinctive traditions, but they acknowledge the Pope as their head, and their members are just as Catholic as the members of the Latin Church, which is by far the biggest division of the Catholic Church, and the one most people are familiar with.

St. Alphonsa's aunt, who brought her up after the death of her mother, wished her to get married. She had many suitors. St. Alphonsa wished to join the Carmelite order, and in order to escape marriage, she put her foot into a fire. She had read about similar feats by saints who had also wished to escape marriage. The fire burned her more seriously that she had expected, but her aunt continued to plan a match for her. In the end, she told her father that she would rather die than marry, and the plans were abandoned. She eventually joined the Clarist Sisters of Malabar, taught girls, and gained a reputation for prophecy. She also had the power to understand languages she had never learned. When she died, crowds of people visited her tomb.

A more recent saint — St. María de las Maravillas Pidal Chico de Guzmán, who died in 1974 at the age of 83, and who founded many Carmelite monasteries in Spain and India — was even more precocious when it came to vowing virginity. She took a private vow of virginity when she was only five years old.

The Church celebrates several saints who are "martyrs in defense of chastity." St. Maria Goretti (1890–1902) may be the most famous of these martyrs — she died at the age of eleven, defending her virginity against the son of a family who shared accommodation with her own family. St. Maria was a saintly child, in her life as well as her death. She prayed constantly, and taught other children prayers and Bible stories. Once, when a shopkeeper gave her an apple as a gift for herself, she put it into her bag and told him she was keeping it for her "brother" Alessandro (the young man who eventually assaulted her). When he gave her a biscuit, she also put that in her bag and said she would keep it for her sister. In the end, the shopkeeper had to insist that she eat a biscuit in front of her, to ensure that she took something for herself.

By the time Alessandro assaulted her, he was almost twenty and had already been making advances to her, which she had resisted. She began to avoid him, so he waited until she was alone in the house before he made his move. (As her family were farm laborers, this was not too difficult.) This is how Ann Ball describes the attack:

> Alessandro…returned to the house. He brushed past Maria, went to his room, then came past her again carrying a handkerchief and went to the storeroom downstairs. Later, it was learned that he had sharpened and tapered a nine-and-a-half inch blade. He returned again to the house, and called Maria to come to him. When she called out to ask why, he repeated his demand. She told him she would not come unless she knew why she was needed. Alessandro came out to the landing and dragged her into the house. Any cry she made was drowned out by the steady hum of the thresher going round and round in the blazing sun. According to Alessandro, Maria's words were: "No! No! No! What are you doing? Do not touch me! It is a sin — you will go to Hell!" More than instinctively fighting to preserve her honor, Maria thought even at this time of the sin which would condemn Alessandro to Hell. Although she fought with all her strength, she could hardly expect to hold out long against the husky young man…. At this point, Alessandro picked up the knife and began stabbing Maria. Reports as to the number of wounds vary, but fourteen major ones were treated at the hospital.[5]

---

5   Ann Ball, *Modern Saints: Their Lives and Faces: Book One* (Rockford, Illinois: Tan Books and Publishers Inc., 1983), 169.

Surgery was performed at the hospital, but it was in vain. St. Maria received Viaticum (Communion given before imminent death) from the same priest who gave her first Communion. He asked her if she forgave Alessandro, and Maria said: "Yes, I too, for the love of Jesus, forgive him…and I want him to be with me in Paradise…. May God forgive him, because I have already forgiven him." She died soon after. Alessandro was sentenced to thirty years in prison. For eight years, he expressed no remorse. Then, he had a dream in which Maria appeared to him holding white lilies. He wrote a letter to the local bishop expressing remorse for his crime. When Maria's cause for sainthood was investigated, Alessandro (now released) gave evidence, admitting his responsibility and explaining how Maria had been thinking of his own soul even as he was assaulting her. Eventually, Maria's mother Assunta forgave him too. Maria was canonized in 1950.

Blessed Antonia Messina (1919–1935) is another martyr in defense of chastity. This Italian teenager was a member of Catholic Action (a movement which sought to apply Catholic principles to social and cultural life). When she was walking to Mass with a friend, a teenager attempted to rape her, and when she resisted beat her to death with a stone.

It is not only women who have resisted forced sexual advances at the cost of martyrdom. St. Charles Lwanga and his companions (nineteen in total) were Ugandan converts who were executed in 1886, for refusing to renounce their Christianity—but also for refusing the homosexual advances of the pagan King Mwanga II. Most of the martyrs were burned to death, but one was killed with a blow to the neck; his father was the chief executioner and wanted to spare him burning.

St. Gemma Galgani (1878–1903), the Italian mystic already mentioned in a previous chapter, was pure and chaste to a degree remarkable even amongst saints. Here is a story from biographer Fr. Germanus Ruoppolo:

> One day when rising from the table after dinner, the Devil appeared to Gemma in an impure form and threatened to overcome her at any cost. Gemma turned pale and then immediately ran out the back door to a deep water tank in the back garden. It was winter and the water was icy cold. There and then, making

the sign of the Cross, she threw herself in the freezing water and certainly would have quickly succumbed, had not some invisible hand drawn her shivering from the water.[6]

Such behavior is far from unknown amongst saints. St. Francis of Assisi famously fought attacks of sexual temptation by rolling in snow and thorn bushes. St. Bernard of Clairvaux (1090–1153), reformer of the Cistercian order, was so carefully on guard against even the possibility of temptation that once, when he accidentally looked at a woman's face, he promptly jumped into a cold pool up to his neck. This might seem ridiculous and excessive to us, but it certainly throws our own standards into sharp relief. Magazines that would have been considered pornographic fifty years ago are now openly displayed in supermarkets and newsagents. What would St. Bernard and St. Gemma make of that?

Sometimes sexual temptation comes in strange forms. St. Charles Sezze (1613–1670) was an Italian Franciscan lay brother who experienced temptation from an unusual source:

> Now that I had consecrated my body and soul to our most holy Mother, a terribly great rebellion rose in me and I found myself in a violent sea of impure and shameful temptations; so fierce and threatening were the waves of these vivid thoughts and imaginations that they well meant to swallow me alive, as the whale did poor Jonas.
>
> For my part, I did all I could, though it was little, to stand firm and not to consent to these wicked temptations. I hurried for help to the Blessed Virgin. When alone I used the discipline on myself [whipped myself] very severely, and I tried to distract these thoughts by singing praises to our Lord. Sometimes it even helped to sing popular songs, as I offered them up in my heart to the Creator.
>
> To these temptations was added the occasions of sin coming from an old woman whose home I had to pass sometimes at a very early hour in the morning and at night, always on certain

6 Glenn Dallaire, "St. Gemma's Heroic Chastity and Purity." http://www.stgemmagalgani.com/2009/04/st-gemmas-heroic-chastity-and-purity.html (accessed May 28, 2017).

errands of charity. Though this woman was very old and had no teeth so that she slurred her speech, still the devil put her in my heart so firmly that I could not find peace day or night.[7]

The story shows the perversity of sin. There is something within us which often craves sin for the sake of sin, whatever particular form it happens to take.

Frequently the assumption is made that, although those who have embraced a religious vocation should live up to their vows of chastity, they should also be unconditionally tolerant of the sexual choices of lay Catholics. Recently, the Catholic bishops of the United States reported that half of the couples who enter marriage preparation courses are already sleeping together, so this expectation seems widespread amongst the public.

St. Frances Xavier Cabrini

7 St. Charles Sezze, *St. Charles Sezze: An Autobiography* (London: Burns and Oates, 1963), 14–15.

Two stories from the life of St. Frances Xavier Cabrini (1850–1917), founder of the Missionary Sacred Hearts, show that she certainly did not take this attitude. Both stories come from her time setting up girls' schools in Nicaragua.

When St. Cabrini and her sisters were welcomed in the house of a local dignitary, they were served by native women who were topless. On being told that this was simply the custom of the country, she said that was beside the point, and insisted that the women cover themselves with towels and sheets. No cultural relativism there! Mother Cabrini also insisted that no illegitimate girls — that is, girls who had been born outside of marriage — would be accepted in her academy. This seems harsh to us now, but her belief was that accepting such girls would encourage sexual immorality. Some of the locals were so incensed that angry parents subjected her sisters to a wave of intimidation, even firing guns outside their convent. However, Mother Cabrini stood firm.

St. Padre Pio may be the most famous saint of the twentieth century. This Capuchin friar and priest was renowned for his stigmata (miraculous wounds resembling the wounds of Christ) and his ability to read souls. Many people flocked to his Masses, but sometimes he refused Communion to them:

> He refuses the Sacrament to certain pilgrims. They can kneel three, four, five, ten times before the Communion table. He passed them by. To one man who followed him into the sacristy, he said: "Go away and marry the woman you are living with, and then come back."[8]

A modern reader might be shocked and offended by this story. Wasn't St. Padre Pio a follower of Jesus Christ? And wasn't Jesus inclusive and welcoming? But what charity would it have been in the saint, if he allowed somebody in mortal sin — in this case, a state of adultery — to commit a further mortal sin by taking communion? Because, as, St. Paul tells us, "Anyone who eats the bread or drinks the cup of the

---

8 Maria Winowska, *The True Face of Padre Pio: A Portrait of Italy's Miracle Priest* (London: Souvenir Press, 1961), 25–26.

Lord unworthily is answerable for the body and blood of the Lord"
(1 Corinthians 11:27).

A saint who has an unquestionable aura of "cool" about him is
Blessed Pier Giorgio Frassati (1901–1925). This young Italian man, born
of a wealthy family, was handsome, popular, rugged, and sporting—
mountain-climbing was one of his hobbies. He also had a strong social
conscience, often giving his own clothes to the poor and occasionally
getting into physical brawls with supporters of Mussolini. His family
were astounded that thousands of poor people attended Giorgio's
funeral, when he died at a young age of polio.

Blessed Pier Giorgio Frassati

However, this very glamorous young saint was every bit as intolerant
of sexual immorality as Frances Xavier Cabrini or Padre Pio. One day,
he saw a display of pornographic books in a bookshop in Turin. He
went straight into the shop and asked the bookseller to "clean up" his
window. The shopkeeper did so; however, the next time Pier Giorgio

came to the shop, the dirty books were back. This time, Pier Giorgio threatened the shopkeeper with denunciation to the police if he did not remove them. The threat had its desired effect; the books disappeared, this time for good.

These stories show us that chastity is not just for priests and nuns. Chastity is for everybody. Sexual purity may be one of the hardest virtues for contemporary man and woman to achieve. Indeed, in some ways it is difficult even to truly *aspire* towards it. My hope is that some of the stories in this chapter might have helped readers to see purity as something positive and blazing, as Chesterton insisted that it was. The more time we spend with the saints, the less likely we are to believe that chastity is unnatural, impossible or boring. The more time we spend contemplating the lives of holy men and women, the more likely we are to be dazzled by the beauty of purity.

Losers

St. Joseph of Cupertino ✳ *St. Jean Vianney*
St. Bernadette Soubirous ✳ *St. Charles of Mount Argus*
Blessed Mariano da Roccacasale
St. Benedict Joseph Labre ✳ *Blessed Margaret of Castello*
Blessed Solanus Casey

ONE OF THE MOST OFTEN-QUOTED OBSERVATIONS
on sainthood is the aphorism by the French author Leon Bloy: "There
is only one tragedy in the end, not to have been a saint." Saints are men
and women who are in heaven, who dwell with God for all eternity.
Nothing else that we attain in our lives, if we don't attain *that*, matters
one little bit.

Some of the men and women that the Catholic Church has proclaimed saints were outstandingly gifted. The calendar of saints includes
great intellects such as St. Augustine of Hippo and St. Thomas Aquinas, great writers such as Blessed John Henry Newman, and great
reformers such as St. Teresa of Avila. However, there are many saints
who could easily have been labeled with that most horrible of modern
labels—"losers." In fact, I am including this chapter for the very reason
that this term is so horrible, and yet so widespread. Today, we all seem
to live in fear of being a "loser." But being a "loser" is no impediment
to being a saint—which is the only thing that really matters in the end.

I live in a country (Ireland) where a huge number of the streets,
squares, hospitals, sports clubs, business estates and other public
places and institutions are named after saints. Naming such things
after saints was routine until very recently—not only in Ireland, but
in every country in what used to be Christendom. Who do we name
streets and buildings after today? Very often we name them after sports
stars, rock stars or the billionaire businessmen who fund them. What

a terrible shame it is, that we no longer accord the highest place of honor to people who were usually poor, retiring, obscure, humble and quite the opposite of self-seeking.

Society has always admired success—indeed, striving after excellence is a good thing. But surely it is an even better thing that, above our heroes of athletics and business and the arts, we should honor the saints—who, in terms of worldly gifts, were often very ordinary people. For anybody can become a saint, no matter what their gifts, or their station in life. As St. Josemaría Escrivá put it: "Sanctity is more attainable than learning, but it is easier to be learned than to be a saint." Sanctity is there for the taking, and we don't have to compete against anyone to achieve it.

St. Joseph of Cupertino (1603–1663) might be the most famous example of a "loser" saint. As Alban Goodier has written:

> If ever a tiny child began life with nothing in his favor it was Joseph of Cupertino; he had only one hopeful and saving quality—that he knew it. Other boys of his own age were clever, he was easily the dullest of them all. Others were winning and attractive, nobody ever wanted him. While they had pleasant things said to them, and nice things given to them, Joseph always wrote himself down an ass, and never looked for any special treatment. He went to school with the rest of the children in the village, but he did not succeed in anything. He was absent-minded, he was awkward, he was nervous; a sudden noise, such as the ringing of a church-bell, would make him drop his schoolbooks on the floor. He would sit with his companions after school-hours, and try to talk like them, but every time his conversation would break down; he could not tell a story to the end, no matter how he tried. His very sentences would stop in the middle because he could not find the right words. Altogether, even for those who pitied him, and wished to be kind to him, Joseph was something of a trial.[1]

---

1 Alban Goodier S.J., *St. Joseph of Cupertino: The Dunce: 1603–1663.* http://www.ewtn.com/library/MARY/JOSEPH.htm (accessed May 28, 2017).

Like our Lord, St. Joseph of Cupertino was born in a stable, and his father (who died before he was born) was a carpenter. However, St. Joseph did not resemble our Lord when it comes to a precocious knowledge of sacred Scripture, as we will see presently. Joseph regularly fell into religious ecstasies from an early age, and since his mouth often hung open during these, other children nicknamed him "gape-mouth." Being an admirer of St. Francis, he wanted to join the Franciscans, but was rejected by them on account of his lack of education. His own uncle, who was a Franciscan priest, refused to support him.

Instead, he joined the Capuchins as a lay brother, and worked in the kitchen. However, he could not even make a success of this; he continued to lapse into ecstasies, which led him to drop pots and plates. Eventually the Capuchins sent him away. This caused him such pain that he recalled: "It seemed to me as if my skin was torn off with the habit and my flesh rent from my bone." His own family were not pleased to have him back. In fact, two of his uncles who were also priests chastised him for not trying hard enough. Nevertheless, when one of them heard he had been studying at night, he was impressed by his persistence, and St. Joseph was allowed to become a Franciscan tertiary and study for the priesthood.

Once again, St. Joseph struggled with his studies. He felt extraordinarily nervous about his examinations. However, he managed to pass them through some striking strokes of luck. For the first examination — to become a deacon, which is the first stage on the way to the priesthood — he was asked to give a commentary on a gospel passage. The passage which happened to be chosen was the only one he knew well enough to pass on. For his second examination — the examination leading to the priesthood — St. Joseph seemed to be out of luck, since the examiner was a bishop who was known for asking difficult questions. However, the examination was cut short before St. Joseph's turn to be examined had arrived. As all of the candidates examined had been of a high standard, the bishop simply assumed that the rest of them were, too. It is not surprising that St. Joseph is a popular saint with students facing examinations!

In the monastery in Cupertino, St. Joseph was given menial tasks to do, but his reputation for holiness began to grow, especially on account of the miraculous cures attributed to him. He attracted such a following that his superiors relocated him, first of all to Assisi, and then to other locations. At one time he was investigated by the Inquisition, and at another time he was forbidden from talking to the public. Ultimately he was returned to Assisi and allowed to live as normal.

The most famous aspect of St. Joseph of Cupertino's life is his levitations — he is known as the flying saint. He first levitated on the feast day of St. Francis, during a public procession. After that it happened frequently. It embarrassed the saint tremendously, and his superiors stopped him from taking part in processions as they felt it was a cause of distraction. But St. Joseph couldn't help it. Sometimes the mere name of Jesus or Mary would make him levitate.

In the twenty-first century, many people find it hard to take such stories seriously. But why should they find it hard? I have already written about the Miracle of the Sun, which occurred in Fatima in 1917 and was witnessed by twenty thousand people. If it had happened in 1517, doubtless it would be considered a legend. The same is true of the many miracles in the life of St. Padre Pio, a saint of our own times who was known to appear in two places at once, and to read souls — that is, to know things about others that should have been impossible for him to know. There are innumerable witnesses to this. Why should we baulk at the idea that another saint could levitate, just because he happened to live centuries ago?

St. Joseph of Cupertino was not the only saint who struggled in his studies. St. Jean Vianney (1786–1859), who achieved fame as the "Curé d'Ars" (parish priest of the town of Ars) was a poor student who might never have qualified for the priesthood without some lenience being shown. As his biographer Joseph Schaefer wrote:

> As an inmate of the seminary his career was remarkable more for the piety of his life than for the brilliancy of his intellect. The regent, however, who recognized Vianney's sterling worth, gave him for his room-mate a fellow student of marked ability who took pains to assist Vianney in his studies, and thus aided, Jean

advanced toward the time of his ordination. At that time, 1814, there was a great need of priests and, for this reason, it was planned that Vianney, with other alumni should receive subdeacon's orders in the approaching month of July. But the authorities hesitated. How could they admit to the higher orders one so poorly qualified? This question the vicar-general saw fit to settle for himself, and, after examining Vianney thoroughly, he announced with complacency: "You know as much as many a country pastor."

The vicar-general, however, had previously conferred with the superior of the seminary and had asked him: "Is young Vianney pious? Is he devoted to the Blessed Virgin?" The authorities were able to assure him fully upon these points. "Then," said the vicar-general, "I will receive him. Divine grace will do the rest." Thus, on July 2nd, 1814, Vianney received subdeacon's orders and about twelve months later those of deacon. In August, of the year 1815, he was raised to the dignity of the priesthood by the bishop of Grenoble, representing the archbishop of Lyons, who was at that time in Rome.

Vianney was then twenty-nine years old. The bishop had expressed the hope that the newly ordained would prove to be an efficient laborer in the Master's vineyard. Divine Providence, however, had much more than this in store for the newly consecrated priest, for he was to become a model, whom Holy Church was one day to present to the entire clergy of the Catholic world for imitation.[2]

These last words are a reference to the remarkable fact that St. Jean Vianney, who had such difficulties studying for the priesthood, is now the patron saint of parish priests! His small parish of Ars, a village in eastern France, became a beacon of religious devotion, to which pilgrims flocked from wide and far.

St. Bernadette Soubirous was another poor student. She didn't make her first Communion until she was fourteen, because she had such difficulties

---

2 Joseph Schaefer, *The Life of Saint John Vianney, The Cure of Ars.* https://www.ecatholic2000.com/vianney/cure.shtml (accessed May 28, 2017).

mastering the Catechism. At one period of her life, her godmother would give her Catechism instruction from seven to nine in the evening, but St. Bernadette was unable to remember a single word. Though some of this was down to her tiredness at working as a shepherdess, it seems clear that Our Blessed Mother, in appearing to St. Bernadette, "chose what is foolish in the world to shame the wise" (1 Corinthians 1:27).

St. Charles of Mount Argus

St. Charles of Mount Argus (1821–1893) is an example of a holy man who seems to have had no worldly talents at all — other than singing, which he loved to do. This Dutch Passionist priest, who won a reputation as a healer and a wonder-worker in Ireland, was another slow learner in youth, a poor soldier when he was enlisted to military service (there is a story that he nearly shot one of his own officers by accident), a notoriously poor preacher (despite being a member of the Passionists, an Order which emphasizes preaching), and a poor speaker of English. It was, however, his great holiness, his insight in the confessional, and his supernatural healing powers which made him enormously popular with the people of Dublin. Up to three hundred people a day would seek him out. When he died, an Irish newspaper reported: "Never before has the memory of any man sparked an explosion of religious sentiment and profound veneration as that which we observed in the presence of the mortal remains of Father Charles."

What is remarkable is that Fr. Charles did not enjoy any such celebrity in his five years of ministry in England. It was only when he had been in Ireland some three years that he began to be followed by crowds. One account dates the beginning of this phenomenon to a visit he made to a friend in the scenic locality of Glendalough. To the saint's great surprise, the entire countryside seemed to have turned out to greet him. After that, this following never left him. This, surely, shows that his charisma was a pure gift from God.

Blessed Mariano da Roccacasale (1778–1866) was another holy man who did nothing extraordinary in his life, in purely human terms. He was born of a peasant family, and he was nicknamed "snack-sized" on account of his shortness. He worked as a shepherd before entering the Franciscan order as a lay-brother (rather than a priest). Within the Franciscans, he worked as a gardener, a cook, a carpenter, and—for more than fifty years—as a porter. And yet he was beatified in 1999, and described by St. John Paul II thus: "His poor and humble life, led in the footsteps of Francis and Clare of Assisi, was constantly directed to his neighbor, in the desire to hear and share the sufferings of each individual, in order to present them later to the Lord during the long hours he spent in adoration of the Eucharist."[3]

3 St. John Paul II, *Beatification of Ferdinand Mary Baccilieri, Edward Joannes Maria Poppe, Arcangelo Tadini, Mariano of Roccacasale, Diego Oddi and Nicholas of Gesturi.* http://www.fjp2.com/de/johannes-paul-ii/online-bibliothek/predigten/2188-beatification-of-ferdinand-mary-baccilieri-edward-joannes-maria-poppe-arcangelo-tadini-mariano-of-roccacasale-diego-oddi-and-nicholas-of-gesturi (accessed May 28, 2017).

Another saint who achieved nothing in any worldly sense, and who exhibited no conventional talents, is Benedict Joseph Labre (1748–1783). This French saint, a farmer's son, initially went to live with his uncle, a priest, with a view to becoming a parish priest himself. However, the young boy was drawn to a more austere path; he developed a desire to become a Trappist monk, as the Trappists were the strictest of all the orders, living lives of constant prayer, silence and fasting. The aspiration horrified his parents. Being pious, they had no objection to a religious life, but they worried that Benedict, who was not robust, would be unable to survive the rigors of a Trappist monastery. His uncle, worrying that the spiritual books in his personal library had inspired such zeal, began to lock the boy out of it.

In the belief that the Carthusians were rather less austere than the Trappists, his parents allowed Benedict to spend a trial period in a Carthusian monastery. But a terrible sadness descended upon him there, and he was sent home. He made further applications to this order, and was again rejected; ultimately, the Carthusians rejected him three times. Benedict believed this was a sign he was indeed destined for the Trappists. He set out to join them, never to see his parents again. "We shall meet in the Valley of Jehosaphat," he told them, a Biblical reference to the Day of Judgment. Though he would indeed never see his parents again, Benedict's ambition to join the Trappists would be frustrated. His time as a novice started out well, but once again he was overwhelmed by depression, religious scruples (including a belief that he was unworthy to receive Communion), and sickness. The prior told him: "My Son, God is not calling you to our order." Benedict was heartbroken.

After that, he pursued an extraordinary life of wandering from one place of pilgrimage to the next, living on charity, carrying nothing but a satchel of spiritual books. Although this was a way of life was not that uncommon at the time — many of those who pursued it were nothing more than idlers — Benedict became particularly well-known for the extremity of his poverty ("You look like the beggar Labre" became a proverb) and for his air of holiness. He was so self-effacing that he did not even like to tell people his name. He would receive Communion very early in the day, when hardly anybody was at Mass — therefore most people never saw him receive Communion, despite the amount of time he spent in church. In this way, he became suspected of the heresy of Jansenism. Jansenism was the belief that human beings were so sinful that they should only rarely receive Holy Communion. Indeed, when Benedict was challenged to confirm his orthodoxy, he held back, not wanting to defend himself, out of a sense of meekness. He wandered through France, Switzerland, Spain, and Italy, ending his days in Rome.

Though St. Labre had achieved a measure of respect from many who met him on his travels, the reaction to his death was completely unexpected. He collapsed in the Santa Maria dei Monti Church, where he was buried. Thousands of people visited the church where his body lay, acclaiming him a saint. Soldiers were called to keep order, and the church was closed for some days. However, the acclaim continued. Benedict's cause for canonization was opened the day after he died. (This should be borne in mind by those who criticize "fast-tracked" canonizations in the modern Church.) His life touched even people in far-away America; John Thayer, a Congregationalist minister who was in Rome when the saint died, and who was highly skeptical of the miracles attributed to him, was eventually convinced and converted to Catholicism. This was a sensation in America.

Could anyone be more of a "loser" than St. Benedict Labre? The story of Blessed Margaret Castello — initially heart-breaking, but ultimately inspiring — is even more startling. In fact, Blessed Margaret has been declared the patron saint of the unwanted.

She was born in 1287, in one of the Papal States — small, autonomous republics that were ruled by the Pope. Her father was the governor of this particular state, and St. Margaret might have expected a life of privilege. Unfortunately, she was born disfigured — a dwarf with a curved spine, one leg significantly shorter than the other, and completely blind. Her parents were ashamed of her and kept her out of sight, not even deigning to give her a name — her name was chosen by the maid baptizing her, whose only instructions were that she should not be named after her mother. However, Margaret was a vivacious girl, and showed no inclination to stay out of sight. Therefore, her parents took the monstrous step of having Margaret, aged six, walled into a cell — though, having noticed she was a pious girl, they were considerate enough to give her a cell which looked onto a chapel (at a comfortable distance from their castle), and visits from a chaplain.

If this sounds unspeakably cruel, there was even crueler to come. When she was fifteen, her parents took her to the town of Castello, to pray at the tomb of a Franciscan friar who was renowned for miracles. When the miraculous cure to her physical afflictions failed to materialize, her parents simply abandoned her and passed out of her life forever. Margaret, completely blind, was left to fend for herself in a strange city.

However, the girl's story was not to end tragically, though she still had to face vicissitudes. She was taken in by an order of nuns, where she was popular at first, but eventually asked to leave because of her enthusiasm for the original rule of the order — one which had been considerably relaxed over the years. One can only marvel at a girl who had been born with such disadvantages, and had endured such traumas, being more enthusiastic for a stern monastic regime than the nuns who had taken her in! She also slept only a few hours and used the discipline — a kind of cord used to whip oneself, to do penance for sins.

Eventually, Margaret was taken in by a wealthy family — they offered her a comfortable room, but she preferred to sleep in a garret. She joined the Third Order of Dominicans. From the time she joined, she miraculously knew all the psalms (devotional poems) of the Bible off by heart, which she recited every day. Blessed Margaret had a strong devotion to St. Joseph at a time when this was much less popular than today — doubtless, the foster-father of our Lord was an image of fatherly love to replace Blessed Margaret's own wretched father. She died aged thirty-three, and crowds hailed her as a saint — she was granted the honor of being buried inside a church when a disabled girl was healed at her funeral. It seems poetically apt that Blessed Margaret should have provided the miracle in death that she herself was denied in life. Remarkably, her body is still largely intact — "incorruptible," to use the standard term. She was beatified in 1609.

Blessed Solanus Casey

In more recent times, we have the case of Solanus Casey, whose path to beatification has been opened as I write this book; in May 2017, Pope Francis approved the required second miracle put down to his intercession. This Irish-American priest, the son of a farmer (and the eldest of sixteen children), certainly had a tough road to sainthood. He proposed to a girl when he was seventeen. The girl's mother response was to put her into boarding school, and the romance petered out. He worked as a lumberjack, streetcar operator and prison guard in order to help his family, but eventually he felt called to the priesthood. It was to be a rocky road. He applied to become a diocesan priest (one who serves in a particular diocese) in Milwaukee, but the classes were all in German or in Latin and he couldn't understand those languages well enough to succeed. Instead he decided to apply to the Capuchins, a branch of the Franciscans. Here, he also struggled academically, to the point where many members of the seminary staff believed he should not be ordained. However, the seminary's director predicted that he would be another Curé d'Ars. Ultimately, a compromise was reached; Fr. Solanus would be ordained a priest, but he was not allowed to preach or to hear confessions. He served in friaries in New York and Detroit.

Rather than resenting this potentially humiliating situation, and the simple jobs he was given to do — such as sacristan (the person who prepares a church for Mass) and "doorkeeper" (the person who answers the door), Fr. Casey took his work very seriously. He gained a reputation for holiness. Great numbers of people would seek him out, asking him to pray for them. Even in his lifetime he gained a reputation for healing. People also sought him out for advice. When one young woman told him she wanted to enter the convent, he told her that she was instead going to marry a man in the military and have many children. Although she pursued her ambition of becoming a nun, it never happened; eventually, she married a military men and had seven children, just as Fr. Solanus predicted. The main themes of his spiritual advice were the need for gratitude — "thanking God ahead of time" — and confidence that God can answer our prayers. He died in 1957, and the funeral director estimated that over six thousand people passed by his coffin.

A final story to end this chapter; as I have previously mentioned, Pope Pius X described St. Thérèse of Lisieux as "the greatest saint of modern times." And yet St. Thérèse overheard a fellow sister say this about her: "Thérèse will not live long, and really sometimes I wonder what our Mother Prioress will find to say about her when she dies. She will be sorely puzzled, for this little Sister, amiable as she is, has certainly never done anything worth speaking about." If this could be said of the greatest saint of modern times, how can any of us feel that we are too insignificant for God's uses? So whenever we hear that odious term "loser" being used, let us remember God's "losers."

Humility

St. Gemma Galgani ✳ St. Clement Hofbauer
St. Maximilian Kolbe ✳ St. Catherine Labouré
Blessed Miriam Teresa Demjanovich ✳ St. John Berchmans
St. Raphaela Mary of the Sacred Heart
St. Nimatullah Hardini ✳ St. Crispin of Viterbo
St. Peter of Alcantara ✳ St. Francis Borgia
St. Charles Borromeo

IT IS HARD TO THINK OF ANY VIRTUE THAT IS more attractive than humility. When we meet it, it has all the pleasantness of fresh air, or of cool blankets. Indeed, I have often thought that "false humility," which is so often maligned, is much superior to authentic arrogance! Indeed, one could argue that "false humility" is endorsed in the New Testament itself. "In humility *consider others better than* yourselves," we are told in Philippians 2:3. What, we might ask—*always*? Even when they're obviously *not* better? Wouldn't that be insincere?

Humility might seem to be a somewhat unnatural virtue. Even babies are inclined to self-assertion and jealousy. Even dogs and cats look for attention and get jealous. Boastfulness was almost a virtue in pre-Christian cultures, and it seems to be returning in post-Christian cultures, with boxers, rappers and celebrities of various types singing their own praises in the manner of an Anglo-Saxon warrior. It is time to quote the incomparable G.K. Chesterton again. Here are his thoughts on the manner in which Christian humility replaced pagan pride:

> The great psychological discovery of Paganism, which turned
> it into Christianity, can be expressed with some accuracy in
> one phrase. The pagan set out, with admirable sense, to enjoy

himself. By the end of his civilization he had discovered that a man cannot enjoy himself and continue to enjoy anything else. Mr. Lowes Dickinson has pointed out in words too excellent to need any further elucidation, the absurd shallowness of those who imagine that the pagan enjoyed himself only in a material-istic sense. Of course, he enjoyed himself, not only intellectually even; he enjoyed himself morally, he enjoyed himself spiritually. But it was himself that he was enjoying; on the face of it, a very natural thing to do. Now, the psychological discovery is merely this, that whereas it had been supposed that the fullest possible enjoyment is to be found by extending our ego to infinity, the truth is that the fullest possible enjoyment is to be found by reducing our ego to zero.[1]

When it comes to humility in the lives of the saints, there is such a bewilderment of examples that it is almost impossible to know where to start. So I will start with my favorite account of humility, which comes from the life of a saint I have already mentioned several times already, the Italian mystic Gemma Galgani:

> According to Thecla Natali, Gemma was frequently worried by the street urchins because of the Crucifix she wore, and because of the way she dressed, but she never lost her patience with them. On one occasion in the Via Zecca when she was on her way from the convent she was seriously molested [harassed] by some boys. She was rescued by some people, who then accompanied her home. Although the boys had gone so far as to spit in her face, she remained calm throughout. These humiliations, far from upsetting her, united her all the more to Jesus. "One evening," deposed Annetta Giannini, "when Aunt Cecilia, Gemma and I were entering the Church, some boys began to annoy Gemma, but she was not in the least angry and said: 'By being despised by the world I am hoping to become a saint.'"

1 G.K. Chesterton, *Orthodoxy*. http://www.gutenberg.org/cache/epub/130/pg130-images.html (accessed May 28, 2017).

The outrageously scornful words which were cast at her in the Giannini home by a religious from whom she least expected them, resulted in her love for humiliations being more clearly manifested. "You worthless consumptive and tiresome nuisance, when will you die and cease to soil this house with your presence?" Gemma, far from being upset, answered calmly: "You are right; what you say is true."[2]

What strikes me about this story is that, from what we know of St. Gemma, she probably *meant* these words. Another striking aspect of her response is its immediacy. Perhaps nothing is more likely to provoke our wrath than an insult, and wrath is usually a "fast-acting" emotion! How often have we reacted angrily to some provocation, and then come to bitterly regret it later? The insult recorded in this recollection is a truly appalling one, one which most of us would forgive (if we forgave it at all) only after considerable internal effort. St. Gemma forgave it immediately; indeed, she seems to have been entirely unprovoked by it. Such humility is astounding — and profoundly moving.

My second favorite story of saintly humility comes from the life of St. Clement Hofbauer (1751–1820), a Redemptorist priest who founded a refuge for homeless boys in Warsaw. (This was only one of his many charitable activities.) I will quote the story directly from the biography on the Redemptorist website:

On another occasion, legend has it that he went begging to a local pub. When Clement asked for a donation, one of the patrons scornfully spat beer into Clement's face. Wiping off the beer, he responded, "That was for me. Now what do you have for my boys?" The men in the bar were so astounded by the Christlike response that they gave Clement more than 100 silver coins.[3]

---

2 Venerable Reverend Germanus C.P., *The Life of the Servant of God Gemma Galgani. An Italian Maid of Lucca.* http://www.stgemmagalgani.com/p/the-life-of-saint-gemma-galgani.html (accessed May 28, 2017).

3 The Redemptorists, *Saints: St. Clement Hofbauer.* http://www.cssr.com/english/saintsblessed/sthofbauer.shtml (accessed May 28, 2017).

Reader, can you even imagine doing such a thing? I can't. Both of these stories seem almost superhuman to me. But although it's hard to imagine emulating either of these feats of humility, I *can* think: If St. Gemma can do that, if St. Clement can do that, how can I fail to endure the much milder humiliations and snubs that I endure in daily life?

Another of my favorite saints, St. Maximilian Kolbe, is the subject of another great story of humility. In this case, however, it's more of an impression than an incident. The reader will remember that St. Maximilian had founded the "City of the Immaculate," a monastery in Poland which printed religious publications. At one point, this was the biggest monastery in the world, with around seven hundred brothers. Fr. Lucius Krolikowsk was a seminarian in the "City of the Immaculate." Asked in an interview, decades later, of his impression of St. Maximiliian Kolbe, he said that the saint was so simple and self-effacing that, if you had to guess which of the friars was St. Maximilian, he would probably be the *last* one you would have guessed.[4]

When it comes to self-effacement, here is a story that is hard to beat. If you have ever worn a Miraculous Medal, you have benefited from the legacy of St. Catherine Labouré (1806–1876), a French religious sister to whom the devotion was revealed by the Blessed Virgin Mary.

St. Catherine Labouré

4 Franciscanfriars, *I Lived with Maximilian Kolbe for Three Years, Part I.* https://www. youtube.com/watch?v=l-9X9fqXSBA (accessed May 28, 2017).

St. Catherine, praying in the convent chapel one November evening, saw our Blessed Mother holding a globe that represented the world, with beams of light flashing from rings on her fingers. The beams of light represented graces requested from her in prayer. The Blessed Mother explained the vision to St. Catherine herself. Immediately following this, an oval frame formed around the vision of Our Lady, with the words: "Oh Mary conceived without sin, pray for us who have recourse to thee." (At this time, the dogma of the Immaculate Conception — that is, that Mary had been conceived without sin — had not yet been proclaimed.) The Virgin asked St. Catherine to have a medal bearing this image made.

She took the story to the priest who would regularly hear her confession, and two years later, the request of the Virgin Mary was fulfilled. The Miraculous Mary was immediately popular, and has remained so ever since. The fact that St. Catherine Labouré was the visionary remained unknown. This was her own wish, as Fr. Joseph Dirvin explains:

> In the formal Inquiry into the origin of the Medal held at Paris in 1836, Father Aladel testified that the very first time Catherine told him of the Apparition of the Miraculous Medal, she extracted from him the promise that he would never reveal her name or identity in any way. No doubt it was a promise easily given, because at the time the priest put no credence in her visions. He could not know then what difficulties his promise would make for him later, or he might not have been so quick to give it. But give it he did, and Catherine held him to it. Here again we run full tilt against the enormous strength of her will. A more pliant spirit than hers would have yielded to the importunities of high personages — the Archbishop of Paris among them — that she reveal herself to them; a weaker soul than she would have grown weary of avoiding the increasing traps set for her, and would have surrendered. But not Catherine. She was her father's daughter in obstinacy.
>
> The question naturally arises as to whether Our Lady told Catherine that she was to remain unknown. There is no explicit indication of it in her written communications to Father Aladel.

Our only direct knowledge is Father Aladel's assertion that Catherine made him promise not to reveal her identity. Indeed a command from Our Lady need not be posited. It is quite in character for Catherine to make the demand of secrecy without any prompting. By nature she heartily disliked publicity, and by grace she was thoroughly humble. Father Aladel has deposed under oath that the only reason he could give for her refusal to testify before the Tribunal of the Archbishop of Paris in 1836 was her profound humility and earnest wish to remain unknown.[5]

Her humility was emphasized by one of the other sisters in her house, who gave this testimony to the commission set up to investigate her possible sainthood:

The servant of God was most humble, everything about her breathed humility. She spoke little, and never through vanity or self-love. I consider it a proof of great humility, that she observed the most absolute of complete silence until her death, about the extraordinary graces with which God had favored her. I myself, who saw her so often, tried many a time to make her speak about it, even by laying traps for her. I loved to recite the Rosary with her, in front of a poor-looking statue, which she kept in the porter's lodge. One day I took her by surprise: "Do you think, Sister Catherine, that the Blessed Virgin, who appeared to one of our Sisters, looked ugly, like that Statue?" She gave him a smile, but said nothing.[6]

Even under severe provocations, St. Catherine Labouré's humility was steadfast:

"I remember," says Sister Clavel, in her sworn statements, "that a Sister used to vex her and sometimes humble her before

5 Fr. Joseph Dirvin, *Saint Catherine Laboure of the Miraculous Medal.* https://www.ewtn.com/library/MARY/CATLABOU.HTM (accessed May 28, 2017).

6 Rev. Ernesto Cassinari, *Life of Blessed Catherine Labouré* (London: Sands and Co., 1934), 152.

everybody, even so far as to treat her like a fool, or as a mad woman. Sister Catherine would then raise her eyes to heaven, while a sweet smile played on her lips. One day at recreation, a young Sister obstinately held her own opinion against Sister Catherine. The Superior then said to the latter: 'I can see that you stick to your own ideas very fast.' Sister Catherine threw herself immediately on her knees and asked pardon. 'Mother,' she exclaimed, 'I perceive that I am a very proud soul.' The sight of this Sister, who was then very much senior, humbling herself in that way, brought tears to the eyes of all her companions."[7]

The Pope who declared her blessed, Pope Pius XI, also commented on her self-effacing nature:

> A life given to silence, humility, self-effacement, as if it were almost natural to her, and essential to her condition of life, and which coincided exactly with the very nature of that exceptional woman. Hers was a nature in which shallow eyes would see nothing extraordinary. Everything in her rests on a background of purity, humility and simplicity. It is enough to reflect how, all of a sudden, everyone began to speak of the Miraculous Medal, and of the wonders worked by it, and yet about the chosen soul who was its depository, there is nothing but the most perfect silence.

To return once again to St. Bernadette Soubirous, her own humility as a visionary was very similar to that of St. Catherine Labouré. She compared herself to a broom that the Virgin Mary had used, saying: "What do you do with a broom when you have finished sweeping? You put it back in its place, behind the door." Her humility was again on display when she said: "Don't I realize that the Blessed Virgin chose me because I was the most ignorant? If she had found anyone more ignorant than myself, she would have chosen her."

7 Ibid., 155.

It's not only visionaries who shun the limelight. Blessed Miriam Teresa Demjanovich was a religious sister from New Jersey, a member of the Ruthenian Catholic Sisters of Charity. (The Ruthenian Church is another one of the Eastern Catholic churches, in full communion with Rome.) That makes Blessed Miriam Teresa a "Jersey girl." Jersey girls have a reputation for outspokenness and "sass," but Blessed Miriam Teresa seems to have been quite the opposite. In fact, she allowed the spiritual director of her order, a priest, to give talks which she had written herself, as if they were his own. The day she died he put a notice up announcing that the talks had been written by Blessed Miriam Teresa.

As Ann Ball writes:

> As the priest preached the conferences, Sister Miriam Teresa seemed to listen to them in the same way as all the other novices. No one suspected that the words of Father Benedict had been written by Sister Miriam Teresa. Some of the sisters did speculate that perhaps the words were not Father's own, and that possibly they were from the writings of the saints, but none suspected that they had come from one of their own companions.[8]

Anyone who writes, or who pursues any creative activity, will find such self-effacement impressive indeed. Even the least vainglorious author, the one whose urge to write is the purest and most self-forgetful, likes to get acknowledgement. How difficult must it have been for Blessed Miriam Teresa to hear the words she had written delivered by somebody else, as if he had written them himself? But perhaps her humility was such that it was not difficult at all. In either case, it is an impressive and inspiring tale.

In her posthumously published book *Greater Perfection*, taken from these lectures, Blessed Miriam Teresa writes: "The saints did one thing: the will of God. But they did it with all their might. We have only to do the same thing; and according to the degree of intensity with which we labor shall our sanctification progress. We shall attain that

8 Ann Ball, *Modern Saints: Their Lives and Faces. Volume One* (1983), 293.

height of glory in heaven that corresponds to the depths of humility we have sounded on earth. The harder you hit a ball on the ground, the higher it rebounds. The perfection of humility is the annihilation of our will — its absolute submission to the divine in every last detail."[9] It would seem that she learned her own lesson very well.

We shouldn't assume that the humility of the saints is something spontaneous and effortless. St. John Berchmans, the young Belgian Jesuit we have met already, drew up a series of rules for himself in order to achieve humility:

> To cut short any thoughts which make me have a good opinion of myself, because this is to apply the axe directly to the root of pride, which is esteem of ourselves.
>
> To say nothing which can turn to my own praise, unless obedience exacts it, because this is to take away the nourishment of vainglory.
>
> What can be done in my room, must not be done outside, for the same reason.
>
> When anyone praises me, to feel shame at being taken by others for which I am not. Same reason.
>
> When someone praises another, to banish any displeasure which might arise from envy and to be glad. Because this is a good means of placing myself below everybody.
>
> To desire for others and to obtain for them what is better, and practically to look on others as better, to act towards them in this sentiment of humility, because such is the will of St. Ignatius. Not to prefer myself to any one, to think well of everyone. For if at this moment my brother seems less perfect, who knows if God has not chosen him to be a martyr!
>
> With regard to myself, to hold in horror gratuitous gifts, like that of working miracles, etc. … because often they expose a man to eternal damnation.

9 Nicholas, "Coming to Greater Perfection" (2015). http://thenotsoangelicdoctor.blogspot.ie/2015/10/coming-to-greater-perfection.html (accessed May 28, 2017).

To accept humiliations, first with patience, because this is to augment my recompense; secondly, with promptness, because this is to imitate Our Lord saying in the garden of Olives; "Arise, let us go." Thirdly, with joy, because this is the means of having paradise on earth.

To desire to be despised, and if this is impossible, to be sad at it, because thus I would become dear to God.[10]

At least one saint has composed a similar list. St. Raphaela Mary of the Sacred Heart, the saint who founded the Handmaids of the Sacred Heart and was pushed out of her role as Superior General by her sister and others, wrote the following resolutions during a spiritual retreat. Bear in mind that St. Raphaela Mary had plenty of opportunity to put these resolutions into action, given her own sad history — pushed from the head of the Order she founded, and eventually treated as mentally sub-normal. It is headed "Humility":

To have a poor opinion of myself and to desire that others should have a poor opinion of me.

To receive honors as though they were crosses and to see hidden in them the devil of pride.

To consider myself very honored when, without fault, I am calumniated, and not to excuse myself if I am not so advised by a spiritual and prudent person.

When unjust words are used to me, to hear them in silence and, afterwards, not to refer to them. Our Lord before his judges kept silence.

To speak only when necessary of those who oppose me, and always with extreme charity.

On meeting these persons, never to give them the least sign of complaint or resentment.

To recommend them much to God in my prayers, and not to regard what they have made me suffer but rather the most holy will of God and nothing of malice.

10 Hippolyte Delehaye, *St. John Berchmans* (New York: Benziger Brothers, 1921), 126–127.

About myself to say nothing, neither good nor bad.
Never to reject any act of humiliation which presents itself.[11]

St. Nimatullah Hardini (1808–1858) is another saint who refused honors on the ground of his great humility. This Lebanese monk was a member of the Maronite church—another of the Eastern Catholic Churches in full communion with Rome. He was a director of seminarians who had another saint under his tutelage, Charbel Mahklouf. St. Nimatullah was such a lenient director that he was sometimes rebuked for being too soft. He was known to spend the whole night in front of the Blessed Sacrament.

St. Nimatullah became Assistant Abbot General of the Lebanese Maronite Order, but refused to accept the position of Abbot General. "Better death than to be appointed Superior General," he said. Numerous miracles were attributed to him during his lifetime, and many more since his death.

St. Crispin of Viterbo (1668–1750) was an Italian Capuchin friar who gave advice to bishops and even the Pope, but who had the most menial of tasks to perform as his ordinary work—he called himself a beast of burden. When a passer-by saw him outdoors without a hat, and commented on this, he replied: "An ass does not need a hat." (St. Francis of Assisi used to describe his body as "the donkey," as did St. Josemaría Escrivá; "no coddling for the donkey, only the stick" is how he would explain the rigors he put his own body through.)

St. Peter of Alcantara (1499–1562) was a Spanish Franciscan friar, miracle worker, and monastic founder who was known for the severity of the rules he introduced into his monasteries, but also for the compassion and tenderness of his preaching. It was he who encouraged St. Teresa of Avila, one of the most famous saints in Church history, to found her own first monastery. His own humility was marked; once, the Holy Roman Emperor himself asked to have him as his confessor, but St. Peter begged him to choose someone more qualified.

On the subject of humility, he preached with a severity which I

11 William Lawson SJ, *Blessed Rafaela Maria Porras (1850–1925)*, (Dublin: Clonmore and Reynolds, 1963), 135–136.

doubt anyone of us living today have heard from the pulpit: "Think of yourself with thoughts most lowly. Ponder that you are nothing but a reed shaken in the wind, of no weight, or virtue, or firmness, or steadfastness, or anything else. Ponder that you are another Lazarus, dead for four days, a carcass foul-smelling and abominable, so much that they who pass by cover their noses, and shut their eyes. Judge on your own that this is what you are before God and His angels, and hold yourself to be unworthy to lift your eyes up to Heaven, or that this earth should bear you, or that creatures should serve you; unworthy of the bread which you eat and of the air which you breathe."[12] What a contrast from so much of the rhetoric we hear from Christian preachers today, where the emphasis seems always to be on our own specialness and God's unconditional love for us! Of course, we *are* special, and God *does* love us unconditionally. But that side of the message is incomplete, without the realization that our human nature has been severely degraded by the Fall, and by our own sins — indeed, so degraded that we can only be redeemed through the blood of Jesus.

Another saint marked by humility is St. Francis Borgia (1510–1572). When people hear the name "Borgia," they picture a rather lurid Renaissance soap opera involving adultery, nepotism and poisoning. They think especially of Roderic Borgia, who became Alexander VI and was one of the most notorious popes in history, openly acknowledging children by different mistresses. St. Francis Borgia was, in fact, the great-grandson of Alexander VI. He was a Spanish aristocrat who married and had eight children, but who joined the Jesuits when his wife died. He fled from Rome to avoid being made a Cardinal, but he eventually rose to become the head of the Jesuit Order.

Despite this, he was a man of great humility. When he first joined the Jesuits, his Superior tested him by making him do the most menial tasks, such as carrying wood and sweeping the kitchen floor. He did all this with joy. In fact, it was only when he was treated according to his former dignity in life that he became angry. Once, when a doctor (using

---

12 The Franciscan Archive, *A Treatise on Prayer and Meditation compiled by St. Peter of Alcantara.* https://franciscan-archive.org/de_alcantara/opera/mentpryr.html (accessed May 28, 2017).

his former title) apologized for hurting him during a treatment, the saint replied that he only hurt him by addressing him as "Your Grace." This chapter could be prolonged indefinitely, with ease. When it comes to the characteristics of the saints, perhaps only prayerfulness and charity are more abundantly in evidence than humility. And a good thing, too; since humility may be the most difficult virtue for us sinners, it benefits us greatly to have so many inspiring examples of it in the lives of the saints. In the moment when our pride is stung and our ego crying out for satisfaction, abstract notions of right and wrong often have little power. But if, in such moments, we think of St. Gemma agreeing that she was a worthless consumptive, or St. Clement Hoffbauer placidly wiping spittle from his face, we are much more likely to live up to this all-important virtue.

Catechetics

St. Marcellin Champagnat ✳ Blessed Josefa Naval Girbes
St. John Bosco ✳ St. John Neumann
St. Louise de Marillac ✳ Blessed Edmund Rice
Blessed Cesar de Bus ✳ St. John Paul II
St. George Preca

AS IT HAPPENS, I AM STARTING TO WRITE THIS chapter on the Feast Day of St. Andrew, who was the brother of St. Peter and the patron saint of Scotland. (The story goes that his relics were brought to that country.) The first reading at Mass today, Romans 10:9–18, is very relevant to the subject of his chapter:

> If your lips confess that Jesus is Lord and if you believe in your heart that God raised him from the dead, then you will be saved. By believing from the heart you are made righteous; by confessing with your lips you are saved. When scripture says: those who believe in him will have no cause for shame, it makes no distinction between Jew and Greek: all belong to the same Lord who is rich enough, however many ask his help, for everyone who calls on the name of the Lord will be saved.
>
> But they will not ask his help unless they believe in him, and they will not believe in him unless they have heard of him, and they will not hear of him unless they get a preacher, and they will never have a preacher unless one is sent, but as Scripture says: "the footsteps of those who bring good news are a welcome sound." Not everyone, of course, listens to the Good News. As Isaiah says: "Lord, how many believed what we proclaimed?" So faith comes from what is preached, and what is preached comes from the word of Christ.

> Let me put the question: is it possible that they did not hear?
> Indeed they did; in the words of the psalm, *their voice has gone*
> *out through all the earth, and their message to the ends of the world.*

The modern world is so used to thinking of Christianity as a way of life, or a spiritual tradition, or a moral system, or a lifestyle, that many people do not realize that Christianity is first and foremost *our means of salvation.* Our Lord himself has told us that the means by which we will spend eternity with God is by believing in his Son, by following his commandments, and by receiving the sacraments — baptism, confession and Communion in particular. We know that souls can be saved by extraordinary means — all things are possible with God — but these are the ordinary, reliable means that Christ and his Church have revealed to us. Therefore, it is of prime importance that every Catholic should know his or her faith — that he or she should have some understanding of God, the divinity of Jesus, the meaning of Communion, the importance of confession, and so on.

The process of teaching these truths is known as "catechesis." It's a rather clumsy-sounding word, but it simply means "instruction." It is certainly needed, in our time. If you doubt this, try this experiment — ask a non-Catholic friend, or even a non-practicing Catholic friend, some basic questions about the faith. Ask them, for instance, what transubstantiation means, or what the apostolic succession is, or whether Jesus is God or man or both. Indeed, if you are unfamiliar with the Catholic faith, you may not know the answer to any of these questions yourself. My purpose here is not to make you feel bad about this, but to alert you to the fact that you have been denied basic knowledge on a very important subject. Religious education in most Western countries, for instance, no longer involves learning the substance of different religions. Very often, it focuses more on rather fuzzy notions of personal development and pop psychology. One example of common religious ignorance is the frequent mixing up of the Immaculate Conception (the doctrine that our Blessed Mother was born without sin) with the Virgin Birth (the doctrine that she conceived Jesus without ceasing to be a virgin).

In the lives of the saints, we see a very definite dedication to catechesis — to teaching the truths of the faith.

St. Marcellin Champagnat (1789–1840) was the founder of the Marist Brothers, an order dedicated to imparting religious and secular knowledge to young people, especially those most in need. This French saint was inspired to set up the Order when, as a recently-ordained priest, he was called to the give the last rites to a dying teenager, a carpenter's son. St. Champagnat was shocked that the boy did not even know the basics of the Catholic religion. In the little time he had, he catechized him and gave him the last rites. But he was haunted by the realization that many other souls were in danger of perishing without a basic understanding of religious truth.

The Marist Brothers began with two young men, under instruction from St. Champagnat. Now they are present in seventy-nine countries, imparting spiritual and general education to young people. St. Champagnat once said: "I cannot see a child without wanting to let him know how much Jesus Christ has loved him and how much he should, in return, love the divine Savior." This might move Catholics to ask: do we feel *any inclination at all* to share our faith with others, to let other people know the importance of Jesus to our lives? Admittedly, in our modern post-Christian world, it can be intimidating and socially awkward. But *wanting to* is surely the first step. Perhaps unconsciously, we may have slipped into a mentality whereby Catholicism is "our" thing, and we do not think of it as something that applies to anyone else. Perhaps we congratulate ourselves on not being "preachy." But how do we know that our friends and acquaintances would not welcome some "preachiness"?

St. Champagnat spoke of catechetics in the most exalted terms imaginable, as one biographer tells us:

> Our Pious Founder was never more eloquent, or more pathetic, than when he spoke of Catechism, of the means of gaining children to God, and of the good that a zealous Brother may do. The coldest, the most indifferent, could not listen to him without being moved to form a resolution to teach the Catechism to the

best of their ability for the future: "My dear brothers!" he once
said, "how exalted is your employment in the sight of God! How
fortunate you are to be chosen for such a noble office! You do
what Jesus Christ did, while here on earth; you teach the same
mysteries, the same truths; you do what the Apostles, the Doctors of the Church, and the greatest Saints did; you perform a
duty which the angels contemplate with envy, but which it is not
given them to discharge. You have in your hands the price of the
blood of Jesus Christ; your children will, after God, be indebted
to you for their salvation! The divine savior gives you the most
precious portion of His Church to cultivate. He confides you the
most precious portion of His flock, His children!... To bring up
a child, that is, to instruct him in the truths of Religion, to train
him to virtue and teach him to love God, is a duty greater and
more sublime than governing the world! A Catechism, I mean
a well-taught Catechism, is more profitable than the greatest
penances you can perform; this is the teaching of St. Gregory
the Great. 'He,' says the Holy Doctor, 'who macerates his body by
the austerities of penance is less agreeable to God, and has less
merit in his sight than he who labours to win souls to Him....'
And our Lord, who is Truth itself, assures us that 'he that shall
do and teach' the Christian truths, the Commandment of God,
'the same shall be called great in the Kingdom of Heaven.'"[1]

Blessed Josefa Naval Girbes (1820–1893) was a Spanish secular
Carmelite who made a vow of virginity when she was eighteen. She
opened a free embroidering school which was attended by girls and
women from many different social classes, and she used this school to
teach Christian doctrine and prayer while she was teaching embroi-
dery. This sort of creative catechesis is quite common in the lives of
the saints. Indeed, St. John Bosco (1815–1888), an Italian saint who was
a pioneer of education, used gymnastic feats to attract passers-by to
his catechesis sessions when he was a young man.

---

1 Anonymous, *Life and Spirit of J.B.M. Champagnat, Priest and Founder of the Little
Brothers of Mary, by One of his First Disciples* (London: Burns and Oates, 1887).

St. Bosco founded the Salesian Order, a teaching order of priests and religious (as well as associated laypeople) which is now worldwide. Over fifteen thousand Salesians work in one hundred and thirty-one countries. St. John Bosco was known for his humane approach to education—he said that he didn't remember ever having to formally discipline a boy. He called his more humane system "the preventive system," and said it was based upon "reason, religion, and kindness." He was certainly emphatic about the centrality of religion to the system, and indeed felt he had not done enough in this regard:

> "No, an education three-fourths pagan cannot make sincere, true Christians. All my life I have struggled against the error of bringing up young Christians as pagans; with this object I have undertaken a double publication; that of some of the profane classics most used in schools, revised and corrected, and of Christian classics. Among those I selected those written in concise, elegant style, with pure, holy doctrine, which corrects and weakens the naturalism freely permeating the first. To restore Christian authors to their place, to make pagan authors as harmless as possible, are the ends I have had in view in all the works I have undertaken, and [the] advice I have given, by speaking or writing to the directors, professors, and inspectors of the pious Salesian Society. Now, exhausted with fatigue and old age, I shall leave the world resigned but with sorrow of not having seen the reform to which I have devoted my energy perfectly understood and realised, and without which I repeat we shall never have pupils who are sincerely and entirely Catholic."[2]

Another saint who was emphatic on the need for a Catholic education was St. John Neumann. St. Neumann, a Redemptorist priest from what is now the Czech Republic, came to America and became the fourth bishop of Philadelphia. He was very active in building churches, schools and hospitals, and after his death his tomb became

---

2 Lady Martin, *Life of Don Bosco, Founder of the Salesian Society* (London: Burns and Oates, 1898), 152.

a very popular place of pilgrimage for American Catholics. His views on education were similar to those of St. John Bosco:

St. John Neumann

"The school system of the United States is very liberal in theory," he said, "but in reality it is most intolerant towards Catholics. Every one has to contribute to the erection and maintenance of the public schools, in which instruction is restricted to reading, writing and ciphering [mathematics]. As respects religious instruction, which is excluded from the school, parents are free to have their children reared in whatever religion they please. Notwithstanding these liberal concessions, it cannot be doubted that the young mind is influenced by the irreligious disposition of the teacher. Even the textbooks selected for use are injurious to Catholic children. They are nothing less than heretical extracts from a falsified Bible, and histories which contain the most malicious perversion of truth, the grossest lies against the doctrines and practices of the Catholic Church. The teachers are, for the most part, either Protestants or infidels. Immorality reigns in these schools, especially those which are in the country."[3]

3   Tom Langan, *Harvester of Souls: John Neumann* (Huntingon: Our Sunday Visitor, 1976), 56.

A catechism (as the term suggests) is a book containing catechetics. There are many famous examples. *The Maynooth Catechism* was an Irish catechism in a simple question-and-answer format, one which was used from the eighteenth to the twentieth centuries, in different forms. Those who were instructed from it (I was not one of them, unfortunately) often feel nostalgia for its clarity and simplicity. The first question is "Who made the world?" To which the answer is: "God made the world." No vagueness there! Similarly, *The Baltimore Catechism* was a catechism which was almost universally used in American schools until the nineteen-sixties, and is still used today. It began with a similarly simple question and answer: "Who made us? God made us."

Some of the saints wrote catechisms. St. Louise de Marillac (1591–1660), the co-founder of the Daughters of Charity, wrote a catechism for children with the question: "If you saw a fire prepared, would you be ready to be put into it rather than deny your holy Faith?" The correct answer was "Yes, by the grace of God."[4] It's hard to imagine today's Catholic schoolchildren having such a demand put to them; but, knowing the enthusiasm of children, it would surely inspire them, rather than scare them away from Catholicism.

Blessed Edmund Rice (1762–1844) was the founder of the Christian Brothers, an order of religious brothers which started in Ireland and which counted thousands of members at its high point in the nineteen-sixties. Their primary purpose from the beginning was to educate poor boys, and Blessed Edmund Rice founded many schools which were very forward-looking for the time, for example in the limits that were placed on corporal punishment. Edmund Rice placed a very strong emphasis on catechesis, as his biographer Daire Keogh explains:

> A striking feature of the regime was the priority attached to the religious and moral formation of the pupils. Reading was taught from Fr. William Gahan's *History of the New and Old Testament*. Comments were made on the text and considerable time was reserved each day for "general moral instruction" and

---

4 Alice Lady Lovat, *Life of the Venerable Louise de Marillac* (London: Simpkin, Martin, Hamilton, Kent and Co., 1916), 56.

lessons from the Catechism or Gobinet's *Instruction for Youth in Christian Piety*, first published at Paris in 1665. "This half-hour explanation of the Catechism," Edmund Rice believed, "was the most salutary part of the system." There were set times for prayer; at noon the students recited the Angelus and Acts of Faith, Hope and Charity; at three o'clock the Salve Regina and the Litany of the Blessed Virgin were said, while the day was punctuated by the Hail Mary on the stroke of every hour. Children were prepared for the sacraments and the confessions of the entire school were heard at least four times a year.[5]

When Ireland eventually gained its freedom in the nineteen-twenties, many of its leaders were men whose outlook had been shaped by the Christian Brothers. The new State, for decades, was solidly Catholic in its social philosophy. Alas, the quality of religious instruction in Irish Catholic schools declined, so that a new generation of political leaders were (at first) indifferent and (today) increasingly hostile to Catholicism — to the extent that religious instruction in Catholic schools is under attack, and there are proposals for it to be taught after school hours — rather than being an integral part of the school day.

Blessed Cesar de Bus (1544–1607) was a French saint so dedicated to catechetics that he founded two orders dedicated to teaching the faith, one for men and one for women — the Secular Priests of Christian Doctrine and the Daughters of Christian Doctrine. Blessed de Bus was pious in his youth, but when he moved to Paris he drifted from his faith and lived a life of hedonism.

Then one night, on his way to a party, he saw a candle lighting before a shrine to the Blessed Virgin Mary, and remembered a deceased friend who used to pray for his salvation. From that moment he dedicated himself to God.

Having been inspired by reading a biography of St. Charles Borromeo, who is sometimes called the patron saint of catechists, Blessed Cesar wrote several works based on the *Roman Catechism*. *The Roman*

5 Daire Keogh, *Edmund Rice: 1762–1844* (Dublin: Four Courts Press, 1996), 48.

(or *Tridentine*) *Catechism* was an authoritative book of Catholic doctrine, released in the wake of the Council of Trent, at a time when the Catholic Church was reacting to the criticisms of the Protestant Reformation. This was a golden era of catechesis, as both priests and laity needed answers to the claims of the new Protestant preachers. Blessed Cesar was careful to present catechesis in a way that took into account his listeners' current level of knowledge; he had three different courses for complete beginners (such as children), for teenagers, and for adults. He especially aimed his catechesis at those living in isolated, rural areas, and at people with little education. St. Francis de Sales called him "a star of the first magnitude in the firmament of Catechesis."

St. Charles Borromeo (1538–1584), as mentioned before, is considered to be the patron saint of catechists (along with his contemporary St. Robert Bellarmine). St. Charles was a nobleman whose uncle happened to be Pope, and who gave Charles enormous responsibilities at the age of twenty-three. Amongst other things, Charles was supervisor of the Franciscan and Carmelite orders, and administrator of the Papal States—all this despite the fact that he was not a priest. (He was, however, ordained a priest a few years after achieving this eminence.)

St. Charles was a leading figure of the Council of Trent, mentioned above. The Council of Trent ran from 1545 to 1663. Catholic theologians and bishops came together to respond to criticisms from the Protestants who had broken away from the Church. The Council reaffirmed Catholic teaching on many controversial matters, such as prayer to saints (which Protestants opposed). However, it accepted some Protestant criticisms, such as their condemnation of the corruption that was endemic in the Church. Surprisingly enough, although St. Charles Borromeo was catapulted into a high position in the Church by his uncle Pope Pius IV, he himself took a strong stand against nepotism and corruption.

We tend to associate the Council of Trent, especially the Catholic art which followed it, with "triumphalism." The Council decided that visual art was a means whereby the laity could be educated, and that it could convey the glory of God. Many churches and other sacred works of art created after the Council were extremely ornate and grandiose, as though they were defying the Protestant demand for simplicity. However, the Council itself called for "unusual images" to be removed from church interiors, and St. Charles removed many secular images, such as coats of arms, from the cathedral in Milan (of which he had become the Archbishop). This was highly controversial.

St. Charles Borromeo is also the inventor of the Sunday school. The first Sunday schools were organized by the Confraternity of Christian Doctrine, whose rules were written by St. Charles (though he was not its founder). They were used to teach catechetics to children and adults. It is said that St. Charles was willing to discuss theology with anybody, even peasants and shepherds. As previously stated, he helped to compile *The Roman Catechism*, a catechism that was in use for more than three hundred years. In fact, it was suggested by St. Charles himself. *The Roman Catechism* remained the most popular and authoritative catechism until *The Catechism of the Catholic Church* (1992) was published during the pontificate of St. John Paul II. Both of these catechisms take a similar form, one that was in fact based on catechesis from the earliest days; they examine, point by point, the Apostles' Creed (which is usually recited at Mass), the Lord's Prayer, the Ten Commandments, and the seven sacraments.

St. John Paul II, who presided over the publication of the 1992 Catechism, was himself a dedicated catechist. When he was a priest in Krakow, St. John Paul would teach catechism to students while joining them in various outdoors activities such as hiking. (This was quite daring, as Poland was under communist rule at the time, and priests were forbidden to travel with students.) When he became Pope, St. John Paul gave a series of Wednesday audiences in St. Peter's Square on the nature of the body, marriage and sexuality which have come to be known as "Theology of the Body," and have subsequently become the subject of many books and other media. This, too, was a form of catechesis.

In the year after was elected Pope, St. John Paul released an apostolic exhortation entitled *Catechesi Tradendae* (*The Transmission of Catechesis*) in which he wrote:

Among the adults who need catechesis, our pastoral missionary concern is directed to those who were born and reared in areas not yet Christianized, and who have never been able to study deeply the Christian teaching that the circumstances of life have at a certain moment caused them to come across. It is also directed to those who in childhood received a catechesis suited to their age but who later drifted away from all religious practice and as adults find themselves with religious knowledge of a rather childish kind. It is likewise directed to those who feel the effects of a catechesis received early in life but badly imparted or badly assimilated. It is directed to those who, although they were born in a Christian country or in sociologically Christian surroundings, have never been educated in their faith and, as adult are really catechumens [people who require basic catechesis].[6]

How true this remains of our own time! So many of our contemporaries who may have been baptized, confirmed, and married in a Catholic church do not know even the basics of the Faith — an encouragement for those of us who *do* have a good grounding in basic Catholic teaching to pass it on to those around us, at appropriate moments.

But bad Catholic teaching is nothing new. St. George Preca (1880–1962) was a Maltese saint who was spurred to a life of catechesis when he heard a sacristan tell a child: "God created God himself." This is a glaring error, as God is uncreated — that is, he existed from all eternity. (Even Jesus is uncreated. He is "begotten, not made," meaning there is no point in time at which he came into existence.) Bear in mind that Malta is one of the most Catholic countries in the world — in fact, it is one of the very few countries where Catholicism is the State religion — and that this incident would have occurred in the very early years of the twentieth century, before television and pop culture had unleashed the current wave of secularization upon us. This goes to show that a fuzzy knowledge of the Faith is a danger at all times and in all places.

---

6 St. John Paul II, *Catechesi Tradendae*. http://w2.vatican.va/content/john-paul-ii/en/apost_exhortations/documents/hf_jp-ii_exh_16101979_catechesi-tradendae.html (accessed May 28, 2017).

St. George Preca

St. Preca was also favored with various supernatural visions which confirmed him in his vocation. He gathered together a group of young men and taught them catechesis in a private house, with the intention that they would go on to become catechists themselves. The society was called MUSEUM, at the suggestion of one of the young men, since "that is where you store precious things." As with many such titles, an acronym was invented later to fit the name: "Magister Utinam, Sequatur Evangelium Universus Mundus (Teacher, O that the whole world would follow the Gospel!)."

The new society flourished until Church authorities demanded that it be shut down, pending an investigation — for the very good reason that catechesis is a serious business, and the authorities feared that MUSEUM's lay catechists would teach bad doctrine. Like many a saint before him, St. Preca submitted humbly to the judgment of the Church authorities. (This is a hallmark of the saints. They respect Church authority even when they are unfairly treated by it.) Eventually, the new society was found to be entirely commendable, and given the official status of The Society of Christian Doctrine.

Perhaps influenced by the sacristan's bad answer at the beginning of the work, St. Preca put a very high emphasis on the idea of the Incarnation. He took as the Society's motto: "Verbum Dei caro factum est," meaning "the Word became flesh" (John 1:14). Members of the Society wear this motto on a badge. He also instituted a Christmas "Demonstration in Honor of the Baby Jesus" in Malta, a street procession in which the Christ child is carried, which is still going strong. Finally, he wished every home in Malta to have a Christmas crib, so he would give them out to children who attended classes at MUSEUM centers. This emphasis on the Incarnation should remind us that catechesis must never degenerate into a mere intellectual exercise, but must remain alive to the wonder of the Word made flesh.

Remarkably, St. Preca also suggested that a new set of mysteries called "the Mysteries of Light" should be added to the Rosary—before St. John Paul II instituted five virtually identical Mysteries in 2002, with the same name. Was St. John Paul influenced by St. Preca? Or were they both picking up the same signal from the Holy Spirit? Nobody knows.

In the apostolic exhortation on catechesis quoted previously, St. John Paul also wrote: "There is no separation or opposition between catechesis and evangelization. Nor can the two be simply identified with each other." Someone once distinguished the two in this way: "Catechetics is for people who don't know, while evangelization is for people who don't care." In the next chapter we will therefore turn to the theme of evangelization.

Evangelization

*St. Louis Bertrand ✳ St. Joseph Freinademetz
St. Jean Vianney ✳ St. Rose of Lima
St. Paul of Tarsus ✳ St. Philip Neri
Blessed John Henry Newman
Blessed Giacomo Alberione*

> *"I have come to bring fire to the earth,
> and how I wish it was burning already!"*
> *(Luke 12:49)*

A GOOD TITLE FOR THIS BOOK MIGHT HAVE BEEN *Fire to the Earth*. The saints are on fire for Christ, and they seek to spread that fire. Indeed, now I come to think of it, the fireworks and bonfires of Halloween night, which I mentioned in my Introduction, are appropriate to the Eve of All Hallows for this very reason.

Christianity is not a private belief system. Immediately before his Ascension, Jesus told his disciples to go forth and make disciples of all nations. The command remains active today. In St. John Paul II's first encyclical, *Redemptor Hominis*, he wrote: "The Church's fundamental function in every age, and particularly in ours, is to direct man's gaze, to point the awareness and experience of the whole of humanity toward the mystery of Christ."[1] The Church is littered with stories of saints performing heroic feats of evangelization. In fact, this chapter is especially important, as we live in an era when accounts of the saints are all too often reduced to their charitable works and their prayer lives, and little or no emphasis is put on the fact that they actively sought to convert others.

---

1 St. John Paul II, *Redemptoris Hominis*. http://w2.vatican.va/content/john-paul-ii/en/encyclicals/documents/hf_jp-ii_enc_04031979_redemptor-hominis.html (accessed May 28, 2017).

St. Louis Bertrand (1526–1581) was a Spanish Dominican whose evangelistic achievements in South and Central America were sensational. Louis Bertrand was born in Valencia and wanted to become a Dominican friar from an early age. He was ordained a priest in 1547 and became master of novices in the Dominican convent in Valencia. As a preacher and an evangelist, he seemed to have few advantages. He was not intellectually gifted. He had a raucous voice and a poor memory. However, his preaching soon became so popular that even a cathedral couldn't hold the crowds that came to hear him — he had to preach outside, in public squares.

In 1562, he sailed to the New World to preach to pagans. It is said that he was favored with miracles — initially unable to understand the native languages, he asked for the gift of tongues and was granted it. On another occasion, a native who tried to fire a gun at him found himself holding a crucifix instead, after St. Louis made the sign of the cross over it. Before dismissing these stories as legends, remember the miracles which are *historically attested* in the lives of modern saints, such as St. Padre Pio.

In Panama, St. Louis Bertrand is said to have converted six thousand souls. In a part of Colombia called Tubara, his success was even more astonishing — ten thousand natives asked for baptism. This was the entire population of the place! At first he seemed to have little success amongst the natives of a place called Palualto. However, after he had moved on to a different region, one thousand and five hundred of them followed him to receive baptism! He was not uniformly successful, as he made few conversions amongst the island people named the Kalinago (the "Caribs" after whom the Caribbean is named). This only goes to show that evangelization can be a hit-and-miss affair, and those of us who don't see much success from our evangelistic efforts should not be unduly disheartened.

St. Louis was not reluctant to publicly condemn particular sinners, although he made every effort to privately persuade them to change their ways first:

> Obstinate sinners dreaded the saint's preaching, fearing that if
> they would not be converted, he might publicly reprehend them

for giving such grievous scandal. His fearless zeal was well known, while threats of violence only added to its vehemence by the desire he felt to die for God. An incident of this is related which may be introduced here.... Two gentlemen were giving public scandal by living in infamous and notorious concubinage. St. Lewis, seeking them out, spoke to them privately with zeal and earnestness, tempered with sweetness. He endeavored in every possible way to convince them of the horrible nature of their sin, and to bring them to repentance. All was in vain. He then preached in public, but in general terms, against the crime of concubinage. But this was of no effect. Lastly, finding everything else fail, he determined to denounce these hardened and scandalous sinners. As he ascended the pulpit a heavenly fire seemed to fill his heart and the burning words with which he was to denounce the scandal and to vindicate the divine honor were clearly suggested to his mind. With apostolic freedom, utterly disregarding all human fear, he held up the sinners, who were present before him, so clearly and strongly that many, knowing their evil dispositions, dreaded the consequences of their revenge. This fear was not groundless. So intensely were they exasperated by the saint's reproof, that one immediately rushed forward to cast the holy man from the pulpit. But there was no necessity for the faithful to defend him. God was his shield and buckler. The enraged sinner was stopped in his headlong course by the sight of flames of heavenly fire surrounding and defending the Saint, and abandoning in fear his purpose of revenge, the miserable man turned towards the door and rushed madly out of the church.[2]

St. Joseph Freinademetz (1852–1908) was a missionary of the Divine Word Society, a missionary society founded by St. Arnold Janssen. He was born in the Tyrol, when it was a part of the Austrian Empire. After being ordained a priest, he was sent to Hong Kong, and spent the last thirty years of his life laboring as a missionary in China. (He wrote a catechism in the Chinese language.) He once wrote: "I love

2 Fr. Bertrand Wilberforce, *The Life of St. Lewis Bertrand, Friar Preacher of the Order of St. Dominic and Apostle of New Granada* (London: Burns and Oates, 1882), 262–263.

China and the Chinese. I want to die among them and be laid to rest among them." What an enthusiasm for evangelization, to not only accept death in a foreign country, but to wish for it, out of love for those you are seeking to bring to Christ! The number of Christians in China was miniscule at this time, but today, Christianity is booming (though absolute numbers of Christians remain small).

I have already had several occasions to mention St. Jean Vianney (d. 1859), the parish priest of Ars in France, and the patron saints of parish priests. Although he did not evangelize in foreign and exotic countries, he showed an admirable dedication to evangelization in his own little world. The village of Ars was notoriously irreligious when he became its parish priest; few people even went to church. He visited all of his parishioners, not only once but several times, and always insisted on turning the conversation to supernatural matters. On these visits, he refused to take any refreshment, even a drink of water. Although they were suspicious at first, his parishioners warmed to him over time, and the parish became noted for its piety.

Another saint who was geographically limited — in fact, she never left her parents' home — but who was full of evangelistic zeal was St. Rose of Lima (died 1617), whom I have mentioned several times before:

> She exhorted religious persons, whenever she met them, in words of fire, to go and preach the Gospel to the idolatrous Indians, warning them especially to shun the studied figures of rhetoric, which corrupt the purity of the word of God; and not to be attached to the useless subtleties of the schools, nor to the questions which are therein agitated, unless they may be useful in converting infidels. She sometimes said, in a transport of zeal, that if the Almighty God had made her of a different sex, she would have applied herself to study, in order to labor, with all her power, for the conversion of souls; and that when her studies were finished, she would have penetrated into the most distant provinces and most barbarous nations of America, to enlighten those savages with the torch of faith, or to finish her life by a glorious martyrdom. Seeing herself incapacitated by her

sex from executing this charitable design, as she could not make these long journeys, she had resolved to adopt a child, and bring him up to study and prayer, by the help of the alms given her, and the money she had gained by her work, that she might send him to preach to infidels when she was capable of it.[3]

St. Rose had no sense that evangelizing the native Americans was anything but a good thing — some of the language here is hardly politically correct — but surely we would do well to share her sense of urgency, even if we are more hopeful of the salvation of non-Catholics and non-Christians than Catholics of St. Rose's era may have been:

> Whenever she cast her eyes on the high mountains of South America, she wept for the eternal loss of the barbarous people who dwell amongst them. Her zeal being as boundless as her charity, she deplored also the damnation of the almost innumerable multitudes of pagans in the New World, who have no knowledge of God nor of the adorable mysteries of religion; she desired to be torn in pieces and placed at the gates of Hell as a net to hinder men from precipitating themselves into it, as they do every day.[4]

Another saint who yearned to evangelize, despite living a cloistered life, was St. Thérèse of Lisieux (died 1897). I have tried to be sparing in my references to this great saint, as I feel she has dominated public interest in the saints in recent decades. That is not the fault of St. Thérèse, nor is it any criticism of her. I am, however, rather dubious about her popularity in some quarters, as I suspect much of it reflects the desire to reduce Christianity to its contemplative and interior element, rather than its active and outward element.

Such reduction was certainly not St. Thérèse's outlook: "I have the vocation of the Apostle. I would like to travel over the whole earth to preach Your Name, to plant your glorious Cross on infidel soil. But oh

---

3 Rev F.W. Faber D.D., *The Life of St. Rose of Lima* (New York: P.J. Kennedy and Sons, 1855), 162–163.

4 Ibid., 162.

my Beloved, one mission alone would not be sufficient for me. I would want to preach the Gospel on all five continents simultaneously and even to the most remote isles. I would be a missionary, not for a few years only, but from the beginning of creation until the consummation of the ages."[5] That is what sports commentators call "a big ask"! Of course, St. Thérèse eventually came to fulfill this ambition, after her death — but even before her death, she came to realize that, as a member of the body of Christ, she cooperated in all its activities, including evangelization.

Evangelization is romantic — or at least, it has been considered very romantic in previous generations. St. Frances Xavier Cabrini (died 1917), the founder of the Missionary Sisters of the Sacred Heart, was inspired with the desire to become a missionary in her childhood, when her father would read to his family from the *Annals of the Propagation of the Faith*. The romance of evangelization is particularly vivid in a famous passage from Paul's second letter to the Corinthians:

> Five times I received from the Jews the forty lashes minus one. Three times I was beaten with rods, once I was pelted with stones, three times I was shipwrecked, I spent a night and a day in the open sea. I have been constantly on the move. I have been in danger from rivers, in danger from bandits, in danger from my fellow Jews, in danger from Gentiles; in danger in the city, in danger in the country, in danger at sea; and in danger from false believers. I have labored and toiled and have often gone without sleep; I have known hunger and thirst and have often gone without food; I have been cold and naked. (2 Corinthians 11:24–27)

St. Paul, of course, was possibly the greatest evangelist in Church history, laying the foundations of early Christian churches all over the Mediterranean area. As he wrote in the letter to the Romans: "It has always been my ambition to preach the gospel where Christ was not known, so that I would not be building on someone else's foundation." Others may have traveled further, but St. Paul was "in on the

---

5 St. Thérèse of Lisieux, *Story of a Soul: The Autobiography of St. Thérèse of Lisieux* (1996), 193.

ground floor," and his feats of evangelization are therefore of a unique importance to Christianity.

For many hundreds of years, evangelization essentially meant "mission" — that is, the practice of sending missionaries from Christian countries to evangelize non-Christian countries. However, in our era, many countries which were once Christian have become post-Christian or secular. This is why Popes from St. John Paul II onward have called for a "New Evangelization" — today a Pontifical Council in the Vatican is dedicated to this purpose. What is the New Evangelization? It is an effort to reach those who have fallen away from the Faith, or those who have grown up in a post-Christian or secular culture — those who *think* they know all about the Faith already.

At the time of writing, I am re-reading *Robinson Crusoe* — the most famous "desert island" novel ever written, featuring an Englishman cast away on an uninhabited island off Trinidad. For most of his time on the island, Crusoe is completely alone, but eventually he acquires a companion — the famous Man Friday, a native of that part of the world. When Crusoe introduces Friday to Christianity, his success is spectacular:

> He listened with great attention, and received with pleasure the notion of Jesus Christ being sent to redeem us, and of the manners of making our prayers to God, and His being able to hear us, even unto Heaven. He told me one day, that if our God could hear us up beyond the sun, He must be a greater god than their own Benamuckee, who lived but a little way off, and yet could not hear till they went up to the great mountains where he dwelt to speak to him.[6]

Robinson Crusoe is fiction, of course, but the manner in which Friday is impressed by Christianity is not so different from historical fact. As C.S. Lewis wrote: "A pagan, as history shows, is a man eminently convertible to Christianity." Those who think they have already gone "beyond" Christianity are harder to win for Jesus. This is why we

---

6 Daniel Defoe, *Robinson Crusoe* (Germany: Purcell, 1974), 283.

need a *New* Evangelization, which preaches the same gospel to a new audience, most likely using different means.

This is how Cardinal Joseph Ratzinger, who subsequently became Pope Benedict XVI, explained the New Evangelization:

> The Church always evangelizes and has never interrupted the path of evangelization. She celebrates the eucharistic mystery every day, administers the sacraments, proclaims the word of life — the Word of God, and commits herself to the causes of justice and charity. And this evangelization bears fruit: It gives light and joy, it gives the path of life to many people; many others live, often unknowingly, of the light and the warmth that radiate from this permanent evangelization.
>
> However, we can see a progressive process of de-Christianization and a loss of the essential human values, which is worrisome. A large part of today's humanity does not find the Gospel in the permanent evangelization of the Church: That is to say, the convincing response to the question: How to live?
>
> This is why we are searching for, along with permanent and uninterrupted and never to be interrupted evangelization, a new evangelization, capable of being heard by that world that does not find access to "classic" evangelization.[7]

I could have filled this chapter, and, indeed, this whole book, with saints such as St. Louis Bertrand and St. Francis Xavier, who preached the gospel to people who had never heard about Christianity, or who had barely heard of it. However, the purpose of this book is to *inspire* the reader with stories of the saints, and few of us are likely to find ourselves preaching to "natives" who have never heard of Jesus. The evangelization that faces us is the New Evangelization — the evangalization of family, friends and co-workers who are likely to giggle nervously if we mention sin or prayer. Thankfully, there are many saints we can turn to for inspiration in this enterprise.

---

7 Cardinal Joseph Ratzinger, "Cardinal Ratzinger on the New Evangelization." http://www.ewtn.com/new_evangelization/Ratzinger.htm (accessed May 28, 2017).

I have already mentioned Blessed Bartolo Longo, the former Satanist priest who set out to revive Christian morals and worship in the area of Pompeii. In this way, he is a saint of the New Evangelization, as he was evangelizing people who were already nominally Christian.

A saint who has been proposed as the "saint of the New Evangelization" is St. Philip Neri (1515–1595), the founder of the Oratorian order. The order he founded was most unusual; it has no formal vows, nor are the members committed to a particular mission. Instead, it is a group of priests and laymen who live and pray together, but who may participate in different vocations and callings in the world. St. Philip Neri, like Blessed Bartolo Longo, was motivated by the decline of religion that he saw in Rome. (Remember that this was the sixteenth century. Secularization, though it has taken a particular form in our time, is nothing new in itself.)

This is how one writer describes the Rome of St. Philip Neri's time:

> Religion was at a low ebb in the papal city, which had not yet recovered from the atrocious depredations of the German and Spanish armies of 1527, a decade earlier. There were also grave abuses within the Church, and although they had long been recognized, too little was being done to cure them. Elections to the Sacred College were controlled by the Medici family, with the result that the cardinals, with a few notable exceptions, were princes of the state, worldlings who thought in terms of power and politics, rather than men dedicated to God and the Church. The enthusiasm for classical writers and the tendency towards skepticism, fostered by the humanists of the Renaissance, had gradually substituted pagan for Christian ideals in Italian intellectual circles. Indifference and luxury, if not corruption, were rife among the clergy, many of whom allowed their churches to fall into disrepair, seldom said Mass, and completely neglected their flocks. Little wonder that the laity were lapsing into cynicism and disbelief! To fill the people of Rome with new ardor, to re-evangelize the city, became Philip Neri's life work.[8]

8 Anonymous, *Saint Philip Neri, Confessor — 1515–1595.* http://www.ewtn.com/library/MARY/PHILIP.htm (accessed May 28, 2017).

St. Philip mingled with the young people in the streets, taking every opportunity to speak to them of God, as St. Bartolo Longo was to do in his own time. He dressed well, had a vivid sense of humor (we will hear more about this in another chapter), and took an interest in contemporary art and music. In other word, he sought to achieve that Christian ideal already mentioned: "in the world, but not of the world."

A son of St. Philip Neri who might be even more appropriate to the New Evangelization is Blessed John Henry Newman (1801–1890), who joined the Oratorians after his conversion to Catholicism, and who founded the Birmingham Oratory—an oratory like that of St. Philip Neri, where priests lived in common, and which was connected to a school and a church. It still exists.

Blessed John Henry Newman came into his powers at a time when atheism and agnosticism were taking great strides in England—at a time when it could no longer be assumed that everybody was a believing Christian, and "advanced" opinion was moving towards atheism. Unlike many saints who have lived in such an era, John Henry Newman (an Oxford academic) was an intellectual titan who was well capable of meeting skeptics on their own ground. His *Grammar of Assent* is a defense of religious belief which took him twenty years to write.

Newman was a convert to Catholicism. For much of his life he was a priest of the Church of England, in which capacity he became a leader of the Oxford Movement, a religious movement which had enormous influence on English society—not only in terms of religion, but also in terms of culture. The Oxford Movement was a kind of long-delayed reaction against the English Reformation. To understand the Oxford Movement, we need to understand the nature of the Church of England. Uniquely amongst Christian churches, it is both Protestant and Catholic—Protestant in that it rejects the authority of the Pope and many other elements of Roman Catholic doctrine, but Catholic in the sense that it believes itself to be one branch of the worldwide Catholic Church, descended from the apostles. Some Anglicans have leaned more towards a Protestant view of the Church, some have leaned more towards a Catholic view. Newman and the Oxford Movement took a very Catholic view—indeed, their critics accused them of taking the

Church of England *all the way* to Roman Catholicism. In practical terms, the Oxford Movement tended to put more of an emphasis on ritual, and on Communion. Anglican services influenced by the Oxford Movement looked rather too much like Roman Catholic Masses for the taste of many anti-Catholic Anglicans.

Eventually, Newman *did* become a Catholic, and many members of the Oxford Movement followed him. (The Jesuit poet Gerard Manley Hopkins was one of them.) In response to an accusation that this had been his plan all along, Newman wrote *Apologia Pro Vita Sua* ("A Defense of My Life"), arguing that his conversion had been an honest one and he had harbored no plan to convert during his Anglican years. Newman was a very private man. Writing such a personal book occasionally reduced him to tears. It was, however, a triumph; even though there was a great deal of anti-Catholic prejudice in England at this time, the general view of the reading public was that Newman had made his case, and had behaved with great honor in his journey from Anglicanism to Catholicism.

Newman did not always live on the exalted plane of ideas. He spent much time visiting and ministering to the poor, both as an Anglican and a Catholic priest. He guided the foundation of a Catholic University in Ireland, which eventually became University College Dublin (a difficult job, as the Irish bishops were not very cooperative). And all through his life he was an electrifying preacher, drawing huge congregations. An excerpt from a sermon that he preached in Oxford, as a Church of England priest, shows what makes him a good inspiration for those of us who seek to be New Evangelists (which should be all of us). He reminds his listeners that true Christianity is very different from the banal Christianity which never mentions sin or the Devil:

> In every age of Christianity, since it was first preached, there has been what may be called a religion of the world, which so far imitates the one true religion, as to deceive the unstable and unwary. The world does not oppose religion *as such*. I may say, it never has opposed it. In particular, it has, in all ages, acknowledged in one sense or other the Gospel of Christ, fastened on one or other of

its characteristics, and professed to embody this in its practice; while by neglecting the other parts of the holy doctrine, it has, in fact, distorted and corrupted even that portion of it which it has exclusively put forward, and so has contrived to explain away the whole; — for he who cultivates only one precept of the Gospel to the exclusion of the rest, in reality attends to no part at all....

What is the world's religion now? It has taken the brighter side of the Gospel, — its tidings of comfort, its precepts of love; all darker, deeper views of man's condition and prospects being comparatively forgotten....

Here I will not shrink from uttering my firm conviction, that it would be a gain to this country, were it vastly more superstitious, more bigoted, more gloomy, more fierce in its religion, than at present it shows itself to be. Not, of course, that I think the tempers of mind herein implied desirable, which would be an evident absurdity; but I think them infinitely more desirable and more promising than a heathen obduracy [obstinacy], and a cold, self-sufficient, self-wise tranquillity.[9]

Do we have the courage and the conviction, in our own age, to tell others of the difference between *real* Christianity and the watered-down Christianity that has so often replaced it? Let us take the saints in this chapter as our inspiration.

A saint who has been called "the first apostle of the New Evangelization" (by St. John Paul II himself) is Blessed Giacomo Alberione (1884–1971), also known as "the media apostle." He is notable as a very recent saint who was extremely active in the use of modern media.

The homily that St. John Paul II gave at his beatification Mass describes an experience Giacomo (Italian for James) had at the turn of the century:

At the end of the Holy Year of 1900, James, who had read and reflected deeply on Pope Leo XIII's encyclical, *Tametsi Futura* [an encyclical urging Christians to spread knowledge of Christ],

9 Blessed John Henry Newman, "Sermon 24: The Religion of the Day." http://www.newmanreader.org/works/parochial/volume1/sermon24.html (accessed May 27, 2017).

underwent an experience that would give direction to the rest of his life. On the night of 31 December 1900, the night that divided the 19th and 20th centuries, he prayed for four hours before the Blessed Sacrament and contemplated the future in the light of God. A "particular light" seemed to come from the Host and roused in him a sense of obligation "to do something for the Lord and for the people of the new century": he felt "obliged to serve the Church" with the new instruments provided by human ingenuity.[10]

Blessed Giacomo Alberione

10 Office for the Liturgical Celebrations of the Supreme Pontiff, *Fr. James Alberione 1884–1971*. http://www.vatican.va/news_services/liturgy/saints/ns_lit_doc_20030427_albe-rione_en.html (accessed May 28, 2017).

And Blessed Giacomo was true to his resolution. He founded the Pious Society of St. Paul and the Daughters of St. Paul, orders dedicated to spreading the gospel through modern means of communication. Together with several other organizations (both religious and secular) that Blessed Giacomo founded, they are called the Pauline Family. This is how the website of the Society of St. Paul describes itself:

> Its mission is to "evangelize with the modern tools of communications." It is made up of religious priests and lay consecrated (called Disciples of the Divine Master). They are present in five continents. The Society of St. Paul makes use of magazines, books, cinema, radio, television, discs, cassette tapes, compact disc, internet and all technological means of communication to announce Christ and speak of everything in a Christ-like manner to all those away from the parish life. The models of the mission are: Master Jesus, St. Paul, the apostle who became one to all, and Mary Queen of Apostles who gave life to Christ, communicator of the Father.[11]

The website lists five other members of the Society of St. Paul who have been declared either Blessed or Venerable.

Blessed Giacomo founded a whole raft of publications to spread the gospel, each addressing a particular audience or theme: *The Pastoral Life* (for parish priests), *Christian Family* (for families), *Mother of God*, *Good Shepherd* (in Latin), *Way, Truth and Life*; and *Life in Christ and in the Church* (on the liturgy). He was so dedicated to Scripture that, when his body was lying in state after his death, his followers rested his head against a copy of the Bible rather than a pillow. It is said that he was responsible for the distribution of thirty-three million Bibles in his lifetime! He urged evangelizers to read the Bible every day and to quote the words of Jesus directly in their evangelization efforts. Regarding the use of film to evangelize, of which he was a pioneer, he said: "We need to put down the scissors of censorship and pick up the

---

11 Society of St. Paul, *Society of St. Paul*. http://www.stpauls.it/istit/ing/ (accessed May 28, 2017).

camera." In a poem entitled "Beatitudes of the Evangelizer," he wrote: "We study the ways of the world today and tomorrow we walk them." He once claimed that "the power of the cinema surpasses that of the school, the pulpit, and the press." This may be an exaggeration, at least in our day, when the cinema has been overtaken by other media. But it shows how keenly this evangelizer was aware that new methods of communication had changed the world.

Blessed Giacomo's path to fulfilling his vocation was not smooth. He possesses the rare distinction of being a beatified priest who was thrown out of the seminary! The reason for this might seem harsh; he was an avid reader, and at one point in his seminary studies read sixty books in two months — not all books relevant to his studies. His supervisors thought he was not sufficiently focused on his vocation, and asked him to leave. However, his uncle managed to get him admitted to another seminary. This sort of second chance was all but unheard-of, perhaps indicating that God had a special purpose in mind for the young Giacomo. When he did become a priest, he certainly had no shortage of drive or focus; at one point, when a creditor threatened to have him sent to prison for not paying his debts (his Pauline "family" was growing so fast, he had to build its infrastructure faster than he could afford it), he joked that a spell in prison would be a welcome break! He wrote once of Our Lord, "The sweat of his forehead at Nazareth is no less redemptive than the sweat of blood in Gethsemane." At the same time, he emphasized prayer: "The effectiveness of your work depends more on your knees than your pen," he told his followers. Indeed, he called praying "working on your knees," and prayed up to six hours a day.

One inspiration we can take from evangelizers such as Blessed Alberione is the confidence that Catholics can *thrive* in the technological era. We have an almost instinctive tendency to equate technological process with secularization, to see new media as a danger rather than an opportunity. It certainly *can* be a danger, but there is no reason to be unduly pessimistic about it; sometimes the most liberating thing in the world is a fear transformed into a hope.

During the Second World War, Winston Churchill told an audience of schoolboys: "Do not let us speak of darker days; let us rather speak of sterner days. These are not dark days; these are great days — the greatest days our country has ever lived." Catholics today live in a post-Christian society, where to be a Catholic is to swim against the tide. But let us bear in mind the words of G.K. Chesterton: "A dead thing can go with the stream, but only a living thing can go against it." Saints of the past had to sail to faraway countries to be missionaries. We only have to step outside our front door. What an opportunity we have to be heroes, to be saints — to be New Evangelists!

The Eucharist

Blessed John Henry Newman ✳ *St. Peter Julian Eymard*
St. Mary Euphrasia Pelletier ✳ *St. Rose of Lima*
St. Alphonsus Liguori ✳ *St. John Berchmans*
St. Pius X ✳ *St. Jean Baptiste de La Salle*
St. Bernadette Soubirous ✳ *St. Gemma Galgani*
Blessed Alexandrina Maria da Costa
St. Margaret Mary Alacoque

EVERY DAY, HUNDREDS OF THOUSANDS OF MASSES
are celebrated all over the world. The climax of the Mass is the moment
when the priest holds his hands over the bread and wine and says
some variation of these words: "On the day before he was to suffer
he took bread in his holy and venerable hands, and with eyes raised
to heaven to you, O God, his almighty Father, giving you thanks, he
said the blessing, broke the bread and gave it to his disciples, saying:
Take this, all of you, and eat of it; for this is my body, which will be
given up for you." At that moment, the communion wafer becomes the
body and blood of our Lord Jesus Christ. This is the central mystery
of our Faith; what the Second Vatican Council called "the source and
summit" of the spiritual life.

The Real Presence in the Eucharist — the doctrine that Christ is
"really, truly and substantially" present in the Eucharist — has been
controversial through the entire history of the Catholic Church. Indeed,
it was controversial even during the lifetime of Jesus. In this famous
passage from the sixth chapter of John's gospel, our Lord introduces
his listeners to the idea of the Eucharist:

> "Whoever eats my flesh and drinks my blood has eternal life, and
> I will raise him on the last day. For my flesh is true food, and my

blood is true drink. Whoever eats my flesh and drinks my blood remains in me and I in him." These things he said while teaching in the synagogue in Capernaum.

Then many of his disciples who were listening said, "This saying is hard; who can accept it?" Since Jesus knew that his disciples were murmuring about this, he said to them, "Does this shock you? What if you were to see the Son of Man ascending to where he was before? It is the spirit that gives life, while the flesh is of no avail. The words I have spoken to you are spirit and life. But there are some of you who do not believe." Jesus knew from the beginning the ones who would not believe and the one who would betray him. And he said, "For this reason I have told you that no one can come to me unless it is granted him by my Father."

As a result of this, many of his disciples returned to their former way of life and no longer accompanied him.

We might sympathize with those disciples, since what Jesus was proposing sounded like cannibalism. Perhaps they had visions of Jesus being sliced up and eaten piece by piece. However, the idea that blood and wine is transformed into Jesus is hardly less bizarre, and it's perhaps not surprising that so many Christians and non-Christians have baulked at the idea.

In fact, it even challenges Catholics. In 2012, *The Irish Times* — a newspaper which is not noted for its friendliness towards the Catholic Church — commissioned a survey which found that sixty-two per cent of respondents who described themselves as Catholic believed that the Eucharist only "represented" the body and blood of Christ.[1] This survey aroused some controversy, since some believed that the question had been phrased in a confusing manner. Nevertheless, it seems certain that many self-professed Catholics either do not know or do not accept the doctrine of the Real Presence. Certainly this doctrine has attracted scorn from many atheists and rationalists.

---

1 Carl O'Brien, "Many Catholics 'do not believe' Church teachings," *Irish Times*. http://www.irishtimes.com/news/many-catholics-do-not-believe-church-teachings-1.1063895 (accessed May 28, 2017).

But why? Blessed John Henry Newman, a man of eminent learning, did not see any intellectual problem in the doctrine. He pointed out that philosophers and metaphysicians have wrestled with the notion of what any given object "really is" for thousands of years:

> People say that the doctrine of Transubstantiation is difficult to believe; I did not believe the doctrine till I was a Catholic. I had no difficulty in believing it, as soon as I believed that the Catholic Roman Church was the oracle of God, and that she had declared this doctrine to be part of the original revelation. It is difficult, impossible, to imagine, I grant;—but how is it difficult to believe?… For myself, I cannot indeed prove it, I cannot tell *how* it is; but I say, "Why should it not be? What's to hinder it? What do I know of substance or matter? just as much as the greatest philosophers, and that is nothing at all;"—so much is this the case, that there is a rising school of philosophy now, which considers phenomena to constitute the whole of our knowledge in physics. The Catholic doctrine leaves phenomena alone. It does not say that the phenomena go; on the contrary, it says that they remain; nor does it say that the same phenomena are in several places at once. It deals with what no one on earth knows anything about, the material substances themselves.[2]

If that appears rather high-flown, we may be brought down to earth by the famous response of the Catholic novelist Flannery O'Connor, when someone suggested that the Eucharist was simply a symbol: "Well, if it's a symbol, to hell with it." The awe and reverence with which Catholics throughout history have treated the Eucharist is impossible to square with a mere symbol. If some Catholics do not believe in the Real Presence, very many ordinary Catholics, even today, show a lavish love for the Eucharist.

Probably most of my readers will have engaged in Eucharistic Adoration. For those who don't know what this is, it is very simple.

---

2 Blessed John Henry Newman, *Apologia Pro Vita Sua*. http://www.newmanreader. org/works/apologia65/chapter5.html (accessed May 28, 2017).

The Eucharistic host (the "bread") is "exposed" (that is, displayed) on the altar of a church, usually in a highly decorative vessel called a monstrance. The worshippers in the church then pray before it and (as the name suggests) adore it. They might say the Rosary. They might read Scripture. St. John Paul II often wrote his homilies and other writings during Adoration.

I am constantly astonished at the popularity of Eucharistic adoration. We live in an era of twenty-four-hour entertainment, an era when we can stream movies to our smartphones and listen to music anywhere. Contrasted with such non-stop stimulation, Eucharistic adoration seems the most boring activity imaginable. To an unbeliever, it is simply a group of people staring at a wafer for up to an hour (or longer), usually in total silence. And yet, as far as my personal experience goes, it always draws a good crowd of very ordinary Catholics. I doubt these people think they are adoring a mere symbol.

I will not discuss the various Eucharistic miracles which have occurred down the centuries, and which the Church has approved. A Eucharistic miracle which involved the Eucharist taking the form of human cardiac tissue occurred in Legnica, Poland, in 2013, and was approved by the local bishop after thorough scientific investigation. This does not mean Catholics *have* to believe that it is a genuine miracle, but the fact remains that bishops do not make such announcements lightly.

When it comes to the lives of the saints, we find a bottomless well of love for the Blessed Eucharist. St. Peter Julian Eymard (1811–1868) was a French saint who loved the Eucharist so much that he formed a religious congregation entirely devoted to it, the Congregation of the Blessed Sacrament. St. Eymard had considerable trouble getting the Congregation started. He first had to be released from his vows as a member of the Marist Order (another religious congregation), and new recruits came very slowly. However, he had a very definite vision of what the Blessed Eucharist deserved, as biographer Edward Tenaillion explains:

> God, annihilated as He is in the Sacrament of His love, has as
> King of Heaven and earth, a right to a solemn and perpetual

worship which, according to the feeble conception of this world, should correspond to the glory of Heaven, but which He willed to sacrifice in order to dwell among men. But Christians cannot neglect the duties of their state in life without disarranging the good order of society. Pere Eymard's idea was to gather together some men of good will and free from worldly cares, who would form the earthy court of the Heavenly King. Then the Lord would come forth from his tabernacle to manifest himself and reign. He would be the Master, and He would have servants destined for His service alone, for His Divine person.[3]

St. Peter Julian Eymard

In a previous chapter we saw how St. Thérèse of Lisieux realized that, being a member of the Church, she had a part in all the vocations that

---

3 Rev. Edmond Tenaillon, *Venerable Pierre Julien Eymard the Priest of the Eucharist, Founder of the Congregations of the Fathers of the Blessed Sacrament* (New York: Sentinel Press, 1914), 37–38.

were to be found in it, including that of evangelist. St. Eymard made the same point to his followers, and the point is especially relevant when we consider that that the Eucharist is the "source and summit" of the Church's whole life:

> The Lord has different classes of servants. Some labor afar for His glory, while others He desires to be attracted to His glorious service alone. He has invited you to follow Him, but it is He alone that you must seek, and it is also from Him alone that you must expect everything.... Just as he attaches his apostles to His mission, He has bound you to his Person. Your duty is to be constantly before Jesus in the Sacrament of the Altar. If ever the Blessed Sacrament ceased to exist, we too should no longer have any motive to exist. It is by Adoration that the Society of the Most Blessed Sacrament responds to God's designs over it. Adoration! Nothing can take its place, and everything else must give way to this, our first duty. In order to be wholly attached to the service of the Heavenly King and always prepared to fulfill the end of their vocation of adorers, our Religious will preserve their independence, their liberty, by not engaging in any other service.[4]

As a matter of fact, the Congregation of the Blessed Sacrament do engage in various ministries, but they are always focused on the Eucharist.

Doesn't Adoration get boring, though? This was St. Eymard's response to this suggestion:

> But what should be the subject of that Adoration which comes around so often? Routine deadens. Would you know the secret of meditation on the Blessed Sacrament? Look through the prism of this Divine Mystery at all the truths, all the virtues of religion.
>
> What more simple than to find a likeness between Jesus' birth in the stable of Bethlehem and this sacramental birth on the altar

4 Ibid., 39.

and in our heart? Who does not understand that the hidden life at Nazareth is continued in the Sacred Host of the tabernacle, and that the Passion which the man-God endured on Calvary is daily renewed at the Holy Sacrifice of the Mass? Is not the Lord meek and humble of heart in the Blessed Sacrament as He was during his mortal life? Is He not always the Good Shepherd, the Divine Consoler, the Friend of all hearts? Happy the soul that knows how to find Jesus in the Blessed Sacrament, and in the Blessed Sacrament all things![5]

St. Mary Euphrasia Pelletier (1796–1868) is a saint about whom you have probably never heard. She was a Frenchwoman who founded the Congregation of our Lady of Charity of the Good Shepherd (or, more familiarly, the Sisters of the Good Shepherd). The order was founded to help girls who were in difficulty — whether they were orphaned, homeless, or had turned to prostitution. By the time she died, the order had over two thousand professed sisters. One of the tasks of the Congregation was to make communion wafers. St. Pelletier's love of the Eucharist is extravagantly expressed in one biography:

> She did not separate meditation from Holy Communion, for she judged that they supplemented one another. Her own devotion to the Blessed Eucharist was beyond expression. Holy Communion was the life of her life from which she drew superhuman strength and heavenly delight. "With the Blessed Sacrament and souls to save," she said, "I would willingly consent to be deprived of the eternal reward for many long years." The thought of a sacrilege was unbearable to her. Telling the novices on day that the ciborium with the Sacred Hosts had been stolen from St. James's Church, she exclaimed in a transport of love: "If the Sacred Hosts were found even in a gutter, how happy I would be to consume them immediately if I were allowed!"[6]

---

5 Ibid., 42–43.
6 Gaetan Bernoville, *Saint Mary Euphrasia Pelletier: Foundress of the Good Shepherd Sisters* (Dublin: Clonmore and Reynolds, 1959), 85.

Another example of extravagant love for the Eucharist comes from St. Rose of Lima, whom I have mentioned so often before in this book:

> On the eve of her Communion, she fasted rigorously on bread and water usually, and took the discipline to blood [scourged herself till she bled], and by these austerities she sought to imitate Jesus Christ her spouse, who is as a victim immolated in this mystery. She had also the custom of preparing her heart for him by a number of ejaculatory prayers, which she used to express the loving impatience she felt to possess Him; in a word, she disposed herself as carefully for each Communion, as if she were going to enjoy that happiness for the last time in her life.[7]

Few of us will scourge ourselves until we bleed before receiving Communion. But preparing ourselves for each Communion as though it is going to be our last is surely a good example.

Many people, when they go to Mass, leave the church immediately after the final blessing, or even immediately after they receive Communion. It would be wrong to judge any particular person who does this, as they may have a good reason. I myself have frequently had to leave Mass in a hurry, needing to be somewhere else immediately. However, the ideal is to spend some time in prayerful thanksgiving for receiving Holy Communion. A famous story tells of St. Philip Neri — the founder of the Oratorians who we met in the last chapter — sending two altar boys holding candles to follow a man who left the church immediately after receiving Holy Communion. When the man returned to ask the purpose of this, St. Philip Neri told him that, since he refused to adore Jesus after receiving him in Communion, the altar boys were there to do it for him. I doubt the man was in any hurry to leave after that.

To return to St. Rose of Lima, her own thanksgiving after Communion was supernaturally intense:

---

7 Rev F.W. Faber D.D., *The Life of St. Rose of Lima* (New York: P.J. Kennedy and Sons, 1855), 42.

She was often surrounded by light at the altar; sometimes she seemed to possess a superhuman beauty; and those who noticed this change would have taken her for an angel, had not her face assumed its ordinary expression; and many religious persons have said that they saw issue from her eyes, from her hands, and from almost every part of her body, rays as brilliant as those of the sun, when she was making her thanksgiving after Communion.[8]

She was also an enthusiast for Eucharistic adoration:

When the forty hours' prayer was taking place in any church, she went thither, and remained motionless before the most holy Sacrament, completely absorbed in God from morning to night.... The following was her method of proceeding during the Octave of the most blessed Sacrament, and the manner in which she spent the four last years of her life. She was not satisfied with accompanying the Beloved in her heart in procession and the Sepulchre on Maundy Thursday; she remained in his company for twenty-four hours, with such profound respect that she dared not sit, nor even lean ever so little against the wall to support her extreme weakness.[9]

(The "forty hours' prayer" is an extended form of Eucharistic adoration, while Maundy Thursday is the day before Good Friday, a day on which the Eucharist is moved to an "altar of repose.")

The saints longed to meet Jesus in the Eucharist. A Doctor of the Church, St. Alphonsus Liguori (died 1787), believed that Jesus also longed to meet *us* in the Eucharist, and that this is the explanation of a gospel passage which might seem a bit puzzling otherwise:

The hour which Jesus called "his hour" was the hour of that night in which His Passion [suffering] was to begin. But why he call so sad an hour his hour? Because this was the hour for which

8 Ibid., 143.
9 Ibid., 145.

he had sighed during his whole life, having determined to leave us in this night the Holy Communion, by which he desired to unite himself entirely to the soul, whom he loved and for whom he was soon to give his blood and his life. Behold how he spoke on that night to his disciples. "With desire have I desired to eat this Pasch [Passover meal] with you." By which words he would express to us the desire and anxiety that he had to unite himself to us in this Sacrament of love. "With desire have I desired"; these words, said St. Laurence Justinian, were words which came from the heart of Jesus, which was burning with infinite love: "This is the voice of the most ardent charity."[10]

We have already met St. John Berchmans, the Jesuit seminarian who died at the age of twenty-two and was one of the outstandingly pious children I discussed in the chapter on childhood. His devotion to the Eucharist was no less notable:

> He goes to the chapel seven times a day to adore the Blessed Sacrament and being unable to prolong his visits as far as he would have liked, he begs St. Aloysius and St. Stanislaus to take his place till he comes back. It was a joy for him to see that a good number of his companions imitated his example by going to kneel before the tabernacle before retiring for the night. This pious practice became general in the province of Belgian Flanders, and is observed there to this day.[11]

Many Catholics throughout history have been inhibited from frequently receiving Communion through a misguided notion of reverence towards the Blessed Sacrament. Today, Catholics who are in a state of grace (that is, not guilty of any unconfessed mortal sins) are encouraged to receive Communion daily if possible. But this was not always the case, as the *Catholic Encyclopedia* explains:

10 St. Alphonsus de Liguori, *The Holy Eucharist: The Sacrifice, the Sacrament, and the Sacred Heart of Jesus Christ* (New York: Benziger, 1887), 222.

11 Hippolyte Delehaye, *St. John Berchmans* (New York: Benziger Brothers, 1921), 49.

Strange to say, it was in the Middle Ages, "the Ages of Faith," that Communion was less frequent than at any other period of the Church's history. The Fourth Lateran Council compelled the faithful, under pain of excommunication, to receive at least once a year. The Poor Clares, by rule, communicated six times a year; the Dominicanesses, fifteen times; the Third Order of St. Dominic, four times. Even saints received rarely: St. Louis six times a year, St. Elizabeth only three times.[12]

In the seventeenth and eighteenth centuries, a movement within the Catholic Church called Jansenism, which put an excessive emphasis on human sinfulness, discouraged Catholics from frequent Communion. It held that nobody should receive Communion unless they had reached a high standard of spiritual perfection. Eventually it was suppressed by the Popes, but long after its disappearance its after-effects lingered. This also helped to discourage Catholics from frequent Communion.

One Pope who did a great deal to promote daily Communion was St. Pius X, whose birth-name was Giussepe Sarto (1835–1914). He was the son of a postman. He grew up in poverty, and he lived a simple and spartan life even as Pope. Pius X was a staunch defender of Catholic orthodoxy, uncompromising in his condemnation of "modernists" who wished to water down the Faith, or cast doubt on its dogmas. When it came to Communion, however, he was a "liberal" in the sense that he wished all Catholics in a state of grace to receive it frequently. He called it "the surest and safest way to Heaven." Indeed, he even lowered the age at which it could be received from twelve to seven.

A charming story demonstrates Pope Pius's eagerness that even young children should receive Communion:

Pope Piux X believed any baptized child should be allowed to receive Communion when he understood the difference between the Eucharist and ordinary bread. Full reason was not necessary — "incipient reason" was enough. Once an Englishman

12 Thomas Scannell, "Frequent Communion." http://www.newadvent.org/cathen/06278a. htm (accessed May 28, 2017).

brought his son to a private audience with him and the Pope asked how old he was. The man said he was four years old and hoped to make his Communion soon. Pope Pius said, "Well, let us see what he knows," and asked these questions:

"Whom do you receive in Holy Communion, my child?"

"Jesus Christ."

"And who is Jesus Christ."

"He is God."

The Pope said, "Bring him to my Mass tomorrow morning and I will give him Holy Communion myself."[13]

St. Pope Pius X

St. Jean-Baptiste de La Salle (1651–1719), a French priest and educational reformer, addressed those who feared they were unworthy to receive frequent Communion in his *Meditations*:

13 Katherine Burton, *The Great Mantle: The Life of Giuseppe Melchiore Sarto, Pope Pius X* (Dublin: Clonmore and Reynolds, 1950), 194–195.

Some say that they are not worthy to communicate often. They must not ever expect to be worthy; everybody, no matter who they are, must acknowledge their unworthiness to approach this sacrament. You may say that this sacrament contains Sanctity itself, and therefore it requires a great deal of holiness in those who receive it frequently. To talk in this fashion is to consider as preparation for the sacrament what is really its effect. We communicate not because we are holy, but in order to become so.[14]

St. Bernadette Soubirous was once asked what made her happier — seeing our Blessed Lady, or receiving Communion? Her reply was: "I don't know; those two things go together and can't be compared. All I know is that I was intensely happy in both cases."[15]

The Catholic writer Vinny Flynn, in an excellent little book entitled *7 Secrets of the Eucharist*, recommends the practice of "spiritual Communion." Spiritual Communion is the act whereby we ardently desire Communion. It is often recommended to those who cannot receive sacramentally — perhaps they are unable to attend Mass that day. But as Flynn emphasizes: "Spiritual Communion is not a substitute for sacramental Communion, but a very real anticipation and extension of its fruits." He quotes two saints who were devotees of the practice:

St. Francis de Sales resolved to make a spiritual Communion at least every fifteen minutes so that he could link all the events of the day to his reception of the Eucharist at Mass.

St. Maximilian Kolbe, in his addition to his reception of the Eucharist, made frequent visits to the Blessed Sacrament, often more than ten times a day. But even this was not enough for him, so, like St. Francis de Sales, he resolved to enter into spiritual Communion "at least once every quarter hour."[16]

14 W.J. Battersby, *De La Salle: Saint and Spiritual Writer* (London: Longmans Green, 1950), 102.

15 Francis Trochu, *Saint Bernadette Soubirous* (London: Longman, Greens and Co., 1957), 190.

16 Vinny Flynn, *7 Secrets of the Eucharist* (Stockbridge, Massachusetts: MercySong, 1987), 86.

However, Flynn emphasizes again: "There can be no substitute for regular sacramental Communion, and our spiritual Communion must always have sacramental Communion as its goal."

St. Gemma Galgani, one of my favorite saints, has already featured heavily in this book, but it would seem unfair not to include her in this chapter. The Eucharist was the center of her life, and she yearned for it all the time. Missing Mass, even when she had a very good reason, caused her torments:

> After all that has been said of the hunger and thirst of this fervent Soul for the Blessed Sacrament, it is easy to understand what a terrible affliction it must have been for her not to be able to go to the Church for Holy Communion. This occurred but very seldom and only when she was dangerously ill. She prayed and besought our Lord to make her well enough to get up, and if He willed her to suffer, that her pains might be increased a hundredfold and she would willingly accept them, "rather than remain (these are her words) deprived of the Bread of Life."
>
> And in order to prevail with Him more surely she added: "To an ardent Lover as You art O Lord, so many entreaties are not needed; He understands at the first word. Then say yes, and I come." And as a rule that most ardent Lover said yes, and Gemma strengthened by her great faith was able to rise, although a little time before her temperature had gone up to 104 degrees. When, however, Our Lord disposed otherwise, this good child bowed her head saying, "Fiat [so be it]" and contented herself with a spiritual Communion only.
>
> In this as well, the spiritual communications she received were so many and such, that they amply repaid her for the sensible privation of the Divine Food.[17]

The Portuguese mystic Blessed Alexandrina Maria da Costa (1904–1955) had such a devotion to the Eucharist that she ate no other food

---

17 Venerable Reverend Germanus C.P., *The Life of the Servant of God Gemma Galgani, an Italian Maiden of Lucca.* http://www.stgemmagalgani.com/p/the-life-of-saint-gemma-galgani.html (accessed May 28, 2017).

for thirteen years before her death. This holy woman was condemned to a life as an invalid when she jumped out of a window to protect her chastity from three men who were about to attack her. Paralysis gradually overtook her, and she was eventually completely bedridden.

Blessed Alexandrina had many mystical experiences throughout her life. Once, after Communion, our Blessed Lord told her that he wished the world to be consecrated to the Immaculate Heart of his Blessed Mother, and that St. Alexandrina should tell her spiritual director of this. In October 1942, after years of representations from Alexandrina's spiritual director and from various bishops, Pope Pius did in fact consecrate the world to Mary's Immaculate Heart, at the cathedral in Lisbon, on the twenty-fifth anniversary of Our Lady's last appearance at Fatima. (Blessed Alexandrina was a correspondent of Sister Lucia, the last living Fatima visionary.)

On Good Friday of that same year, our Blessed Lord spoke to Alexandrina and said: "You will not take food again on earth. Your food will be my Flesh; your blood will be my Divine Blood, your life will be my Life." The saint complied with this demand. At one point she was taken into hospital for observation, and for a duration of forty days was witnessed by doctors and nurses to have received no nutrition other than Holy Communion.

Blessed Alexandrina, like St. Gemma Galgani and St. Padre Pio, was a "victim soul"; that is, she went through extreme suffering to compensate God for the sins of sinners, and to save souls. Her sufferings were not mere theatrics. Some people who have claimed to survive on Holy Communion alone have done so out of a desire for publicity or worldly gain. We should be very suspicious of such people. Genuine mystics are notable for the holiness of their lives, and are always submissive to religious authority. They do not seek publicity. Eucharistic miracles and wonders are not sent to entertain us, but to point us to *the miracle of the Eucharist itself*—to foster what St. John Paul II called "Eucharistic amazement." I hope this chapter has helped to kindle "Eucharistic amazement" in you.

I will close this chapter with two of my favorite quotations regarding the Eucharist, both from saints. The first is from St. Margaret

Mary Alacoque (1647–1690), a French mystic and nun who received several visions of Jesus, in which he told her to spread devotion to his Sacred Heart. She wrote: "I desire but this one grace, and long to be consumed like a burning candle in His holy presence every moment of the life that remains to me." The second is from St. Josemaría Escrivá, a saint I have mentioned many times before. He wrote: "When you approach the tabernacle, remember that he has been waiting for you for twenty centuries."

Prayer

St. Thérèse of Lisieux ✳ St. Josemaría Escrivá
St. Mother Teresa of Calcutta ✳ St. Peter of Alcantara
St. Jean Vianney ✳ St. Elizabeth Ann Seton
St. André Besette ✳ Blessed John Sullivan
St. Teresa of Avila ✳ St. John Paul II ✳ St. John XXIII
St. Padre Pio ✳ St. Joseph Cottolengo
Blessed Ceferino Giménez Malla

THE MODERN WORLD MAY NOT BE INTERESTED in mortification or chastity, but it is very interested in prayer—and this is a good thing. Books about prayer often sell very well—*Calm the Soul*, a book published by the Poor Clares in Ireland in 2014, went to the top of the hardback non-fiction charts in Ireland.

I once heard a priest tell a story about the 2005 documentary *Into Great Silence*, which showed life in the Grand Chartreuse monastery in France, amongst the Carthusian monks. This priest, attending a screening of the movie, found himself sitting beside a young man who seemed like an unlikely audience member for a movie about contemplative monks. Before the film started, the two got chatting, and the young man admitted that he was very interested in meditation. "It's a pity there's nothing like that in Catholicism," he said. "I'm pretty sure the monks in this movie are Catholic," the priest replied.

We all know that there is a massive Western interest in Eastern and "New Age" religions, as people yearn for a spiritual dimension to their lives, and specifically for some kind of *experience* of the divine or the sacred. This is why, even though church attendance is declining in the Western world, practices such as Eucharistic adoration, the Lough Derg pilgrimage, and the Camino de Santiago (a long walking pilgrimage in Spain, the theme of the 2010 feature film *The Way*) remain popular.

Of course, Holy Mass is itself an experience of the divine, but perhaps it seems too "ordinary" or routine for many people.

At its worst, all this spiritual curiosity is simply a desire for a "head trip." But it contains within it a genuine thirst for the sacred and demonstrates a fatigue with the harassed, distracted, over-entertained stream of life in the twenty-first century, a yearning to step aside from the ephemeral and commune with the eternal.

Jesus Christ himself prayed — we are told that he prayed all night long before he called the twelve disciples, and he also prayed in the Garden of Gethsemane before his trial and crucifixion. We are also told that he "often withdrew to lonely places and prayed" (Luke 5:16). This hardly even seems worth mentioning, at first. But think about it! Our Blessed Lord was in communion with his Father *every single moment of his life*, to a degree far beyond anything we could understand. Why should *he* set time aside to pray, we may wonder, when he could have been healing or preaching instead? Yet he did.

In the Acts of the Apostles, the book of the Bible where infancy of the Church is chronicled, we see that the disciples give a very high priority to prayer:

> In those days when the number of disciples was increasing, the Hellenistic Jews among them complained against the Hebraic Jews because their widows were being overlooked in the daily distribution of food. So the Twelve gathered all the disciples together and said, "It would not be right for us to neglect the ministry of the word of God in order to wait on tables. Brothers and sisters, choose seven men from among you who are known to be full of the Spirit and wisdom. We will turn this responsibility over to them and will give our attention to prayer and the ministry of the word." (Acts 6:1–7)

The Virgin Mary, as she has revealed herself to visionaries in Church-approved visions, has always emphasized prayer. To the Fatima visionaries she said: "Pray, pray a great deal and make many sacrifices, for many souls go to Hell because they have no one to make sacrifices and to pray for them." Our Lady told St. Bernadette Soubirous to "pray for sinners." In her appearances to five children in Beauraing, Belgium, in 1932 and 1933, Our Lady was no less emphatic: "Pray, pray, pray."

Outside of the gospels themselves, perhaps the most famous injunction to prayer in the Bible comes from St. Paul's first letter to the Thessalonians: "Pray without ceasing" (1 Thessalonians 5:17). In the lives of the saints, we see how that directive is made a reality. The saints, in fact, made their entire lives into one continual prayer.

Given that St. Thérèse of Lisieux is the most popular saint of modern times, it is not surprising that her definition of prayer is equally popular: "For me, *prayer is a surge of the heart;* it is a simple look turned toward heaven." Even if it has been almost reduced to a cliché, this definition expresses the fact that prayer is more about directing our attention to God than it is about the particular words or postures used. *The Catechism of the Catholic Church,* as well as quoting St. Thérèse's words, quotes St. John Damascene: "Prayer is the raising of one's mind and heart to God, or the requesting of good things from God."

Another excellent description of prayer comes from Blessed Charles de Foucauld, the man of pleasure turned desert saint who we have met already: "When you love, you feel like speaking the whole time with the one you love, or at least you want to look at him without ceasing. Prayer is nothing else. It is the familiar meeting with our Beloved. We look at Him, we tell Him we love Him, we rejoice to be at His feet."

St. Josemaría Escrivá, founder of Opus Dei, called his readers to turn their entire lives into a prayer, and to cultivate an "interior life":

> If God is life for us, we should not be surprised to realize that our very existence as Christians must be interwoven with prayer. But don't imagine that prayer is an action to be carried out and then forgotten. The just man "delights in the law of the Lord, and meditates on his law day and night." "Through the night I meditate on you" and "my prayer comes to you like incense in the

evening." Our whole day can be a time for prayer — from night to morning and from morning to night. In fact, as holy Scripture reminds us, even our sleep should be a prayer....

Our life of prayer should also be based on some moments that are dedicated exclusively to our conversation with God, moments of silent dialogue, before the tabernacle if possible, in order to thank our Lord for having waited for us — so often alone — for twenty centuries. This heart-to-heart dialogue with God is mental prayer, in which the whole soul takes part; intelligence, imagination, memory and will are all involved. It is a meditation that helps to give supernatural value to our poor human life, with all its normal, everyday occurrences.

Thanks to these moments of meditation and to our vocal prayer and aspirations, we will be able to turn our whole day into a continuous praise of God, in a natural way and without any outward display. Just as people in love are always thinking about each other, we will be aware of God's presence. And all our actions, down to the most insignificant, will be filled with spiritual effectiveness.[1]

The idea behind Opus Dei is usually stated as "the sanctification of everyday life"; but it could just as well be stated as "the transformation of work into prayer." St. Josemaría himself not only urged people to pray in a general sense, but he constantly sought prayers from others for his own intentions:

His utter acceptance of God's will led him to stress first the need for prayer, mortification, and work done for God. He was still begging for prayers right up to his death, as he had done since the twenties. He was convinced that this was the most important way to move souls. He asked everyone. He asked his friends and the young people he was dealing with. He asked priests and religious, and also the sick people he looked after.

1 St. Josemaría Escrivá, *Christ is Passing By*. http://www.escrivaworks.org/book/christ_is_passing_by-chapter-12.htm (accessed May 28, 2017).

Don Casimiro Morcillo, when he was Archbishop of Madrid, remembered perfectly well, nearly forty years after the event, how the Founder of Opus Dei had asked him to pray for a special intention of his — such was the intensity of his words. It happened in 1929 and at the time they were unacquainted. Don Josemaria used to cross paths with him at six o'clock in the morning in Eloy Gonzalo Street. One day he stopped him and said:

"Are you going to say Mass? Would you pray for an intention of mine?"...

This was not an isolated case. That young priest did the same with other people whom he did not know at all. More than once in the street, when he saw an honest-looking person going by, he would ask them to pray for an intention of his which was to give great glory to God.[2]

St. Josemaría was perhaps even more emphatic when he wrote: "A saint, without prayer? I don't believe in such sanctity."

When I examine the prayer lives of the saints, I am struck by two things. One is (predictably) the great value they put on prayer, as St. Josemaría indicated. Even the busiest saints found abundant time for prayer. The second thing that strikes me is that, although their prayer sometimes led them to the most intense raptures, saints *very frequently* experienced "dryness" and lack of inspiration in prayer. It's a big mistake to think that saints were perpetually "plugged in" to God in some kind of non-stop ecstasy. The phenomenon of the "dark night of the soul," which takes its name from the poetry of St. John of the Cross (1542–1591) is very frequently observed in the lives of the saints. "The Lord disciplines the ones he loves" (Hebrews 12:6). Mother Teresa of Calcutta (1910–1997) is the most famous case; her "dark night of the soul" lasted decades. However, Mother Teresa echoed St. Josemaría's views on prayer, as recorded in Malcolm Muggeridge's *Something Beautiful for God*, the book that brought her to public fame:

---

2 Salvador Bernal, *Msgr. Josemaría Escrivá de Belaguer: A Profile of the Founder of Opus Dei* (Dublin: Veritas, 1977), 205–206.

It is not possible to engage in the direct apostolate without being a soul of prayer. We must be aware of oneness with Christ, as he was aware of oneness with his Father. Our activity is truly apostolic only in so far as we permit him to work in us and through us, with his power, with his desire, with his love.... Love to pray... feel often during the day the need for prayer, and take trouble to pray. Prayer enlarges the heart until it is capable of containing God's gift of himself.[3]

St. Thérèse of Lisieux is famous for her very frank accounts of aridity in *Story of a Soul*:

I force myself in vain to meditate on the mysteries of the Rosary; I don't succeed in fixing my mind on them. For a long time I was desolate about this lack of devotion that astonished me, for I love the Blessed Virgin so much that it should be easy for me to recite in her honor prayers which are so pleasing to her....

Sometimes when my mind is in such great aridity that it is impossible to draw forth one single thought to unite me with God, I very slowly recite an Our Father and then the angelic salutation; then these prayers give me great delight; they nourish my soul much more than if I had recited them precipitately a hundred times.[4]

So if you are ever bored or uninspired during prayer, you are in very good company and should not be discouraged. Of course, we also have abundant accounts of saints being utterly lost in prayer.

St. Peter of Alcantara (1499–1562) was a Spanish Franciscan friar who was an enthusiast for introducing rigorous rules into the monasteries he supervised. Predictably, this was not always welcomed. He inspired another monastic reformer, the famous St. Teresa of Avila

---

3 Malcolm Muggeridge, *Something Beautiful for God* (London: Collins/Fontana Books, 1972), 65–66.

4 St. Thérèse of Lisieux, *Story of a Soul: The Autobiography of St. Thérèse of Lisieux* (Washington DC: ICS Publications, 1972), 42–43.

(1515–1582) to found her first monastery. St. Peter was so dedicated to prayer that he rarely slept — he is the patron saint of night watchmen for this reason. In his childhood, the family's servants often failed to get his attention because he was so absorbed in prayer. And, later in life, after praying in a particular church for over a year, he could not say whether it had a flat or a vaulted roof!

The Curé d'Ars, St. Jean Vianney (died 1859), was utterly dedicated to prayer and the sacraments. He would rise at two in the morning to say his breviary (prayers that a priest is required to say every day), and at four o'clock he went to the church for Eucharistic Adoration until it was time for morning Mass. After Mass, he gave catechesis and heard confessions. He rarely left church before noon. Then he would visit the sick, and spend the rest of the day in church, hearing more confessions and leading various religious devotions.

Once, a priest who was envious of St. Vianney's success in Ars told him that he had tried everything to energize his own congregation, but that they remained apathetic. St. Vianney asked him if he had tried praying, fasting and giving alms. The priest admitted that he had not. Perhaps St. Vianney had long experience of this being the *last* thing many Catholics try — if we try it at all. This despite the fact that we are recommended to do so on the highest authority — Jesus, when the disciples had failed to exorcise a particularly stubborn demon, and when they asked him why they had failed, told them: "This kind can come out only by prayer" (Mark 9:29).

St. Elizabeth Ann Seton (died 1821), foundress of the Sisters of Charity and the first native-born saint of the USA, urged her daughters in religion to keep focus during prayer:

> Mother Seton told her sisters: "You must be in right earnest, or you will do nothing or little…. What sort of interior life would you lead, if every time the door opens, or if any one passes, you must look up; if you must hear what is said, though it does not concern you? Or, if you remain silent, and in modest attention to your duty, what would be your interior life, if you let your thoughts wander from God? I once heard a silent person say that

she was listening to everything around her, and making her Judas reflections on everything that was said or done; and another, that she delighted in silence because she could be thinking of her dear people. But you know better than that."[5]

St. André Bessette

St. André Bessette (1845–1937) of Montreal was a French Canadian saint, and a lay brother of the Congregation of the Holy Cross. He filled the humble role of porter at his monastery — a role that has been occupied by many holy men — and became renowned for his gift of healing and his deep devotion to St. Joseph. In his life, he had to overcome suspicion, as many thought he was a charlatan.

He was known for his utter dedication to prayer:

5 Joseph I. Dirvin, *Mrs. Seton: Foundress of the American Sisters of Charity* (New York: Strauss and Cuddihy, 1962), 329.

Every moment that was not taken up by work Brother André gave to prayer. His morning Mass and daily Communion were followed by at least a half-hour of prayer. When he was helping about the sanctuary, he made a deep genuflection always, even if he passed the tabernacle thirty times while arranging the altar. Sometimes one of the Brothers would take his place at the door, while Brother André earnestly begged him to so he might make an hour of adoration.

One unsuspecting Brother, newly come and not yet used to the porter's ways, did not warn him, as the other Brothers did, not to stay too long. He waited and answered the calls for visitors and then began to wonder just when Brother André was coming back. Finally, he went to the door of the chapel and found him intent on his knees before the altar. "But, Brother," he whispered, "you have been two hours praying. Surely that is enough." Brother André looked up with pleading eyes. "Just five minutes more."

After fifteen minutes more the temporary porter was back in the chapel. "But Brother, listen, I must go to my classes now," he urged. And then, with profuse apologies, but with eyes shining and happy, Brother André returned to his post.[6]

When he was asked how he managed to pray for so long, he replied: "When I am tired of being on my knees I stand up, and when I am tired of standing, I get back on my knees."

Another saint who was extraordinarily dedicated to prayer was Blessed John Sullivan, the Irish Jesuit I have mentioned previously:

One night in January of 1925, the college plumber, John Gibbin, was obliged to work late in the boys' chapel repairing the hot pipes. When he entered the chapel at eleven p.m., he found Fr. Sullivan kneeling on the marble steps before the altar. When he commenced his work, Fr. Sullivan, so as not to be in the way, retired into a small side chapel. At two a.m. the work was finished

6 Katherine Burton, *Brother André of Mount Royal* (Dublin: Clonmore and Reynolds, 1950), 42.

and the plumber left, but Fr. Sullivan was still there praying. On another occasion the same witness, accompanied by an assistant, was to repair the railings around the community cemetery. Fr. Sullivan came to pray there, and began by kneeling at every grave — about twenty in all. He then knelt down on the ground before the huge stone crucifix at the end of the cemetery, and prayed for about an hour, though an east wind was blowing, so bitter that the two workmen found it hard to endure.[7]

However, as I have previously stated, it would be a mistake to think of the saints as being in a constant state of ecstatic prayer, or never lacking the inclination to pray. St. Teresa of Avila was the first woman to be proclaimed a Doctor of the Church, though that distinction was not conferred on her until the twentieth century. She was a reformer of monastic life and one of the all-time masters of contemplative prayer; her book *The Interior Castle* is one of the most famous guides to contemplative prayer ever written. She is also one of the most appealing personalities in Church history, combining a mystical temperament with a keen wit, and a sturdy common sense.

At one point in her life, this Doctor of the Church found she could hardly bear to pray:

> For some years I was very often more occupied with the wish to see the end of the time I had appointed for myself to spend in prayer, than with other thoughts that were good. If a sharp penance had been laid upon me, I know of none that I would very often have willingly undertaken, rather than prepare myself for prayer by self-recollection. And certainly the violence with which Satan assailed me was so irresistible, or my evil habits were so strong, that I did not partake myself to prayer; and the sadness that I felt on entering the oratory was so great that it required all the courage I had to force myself in. They say of me that my courage is not slight and it is known that God had given

7 Fergal McGrath S.J., *Father John Sullivan S.J.* (London: Longman's, Green and Co., 1941), 157.

me courage beyond that of most women, but I have made a bad use of it. In the end our Lord came to my help; and then when I had done this violence to myself I found greater peace and joy than I sometimes had when I had a desire to pray.[8]

St. Teresa, in a letter to a layman, counseled gentleness with ourselves when we are lacking enthusiasm in prayer:

> Take no notice of the feeling you get of waiting to leave off in the middle of your prayer, but praise the Lord for the desire you have to pray; that, you may be sure, comes from your will, which loves to be with God. We are seeking God all the time, and it is because of this that we go about in search of means to that end, and it is essential that the soul should be led gently.[9]

Of course, there are many different forms of prayer. There is silent contemplative prayer. There are the prayers we say during Mass. There are traditional prayers such as the Lord's prayer, the Hail Mary and the prayer to St. Michael. But one prayer which has enjoyed an enduring popularity down through the centuries is the rosary. This is a sequence of Hail Marys and Our Fathers (along with some other prayers) which are counted out on rosary beads. It also involves meditating on various moments (or "mysteries") in the life of Jesus and the Blessed Mother — such as the angel Gabriel appearing to Mary, or the Ascension of our Lord to Heaven, or the Crucifixion.

There are fifteen traditional "mysteries" in the rosary, and we have seen how St. John Paul II recommended an additional five, called the Mysteries of Light, in 2002, which have been generally adopted. Strictly speaking, saying the entire Rosary would involve saying all twenty mysteries, or at least the traditional fifteen. In common parlance, however, "saying a rosary" means saying one set of mysteries.

---

8 Lady Alice Lovat, *The Life of Saint Teresa: Taken from the French of a Carmelite Nun* (London: Simpkin, Martin, Hamilton, Kent and Co., 1914), 86–87.

9 Felicitas Corrigan, *To Any Christian: Letter from the Saints* (London: Burns and Oates, 1964), 225.

The great thing about the rosary is that it is a "daily minimum." No matter how much your mind wanders, or how tired you are, saying the rosary means that the life of Our Lord and Our Lady occupies the foreground of your mind for *some* part of the day at least. Even if you race through it, it takes time to say it — some people seem capable of saying it in ten minutes, but it rarely takes less than twenty for me.

Mitch Finley, in his excellent book *The Rosary Handbook*, has this to say about the Rosary:

> The rosary is a simple, uncomplicated, nonliturgical way to pray when conscious thoughts and words may fail you, no matter what your feelings or emotions may be at the moment. If you are depressed, the rosary works. If you are happy or sad, the rosary works. If you are anxious or worried, the rosary works. If you are sick or just plain sick and tired, the rosary works.[10]

I well remember the dark time when my mother Patricia died, and especially the last few moments before we finally closed her coffin. This was in our family apartment, following the Irish custom of "waking" the dead with a gathering in his or her home. Before the coffin was closed, a priest said a decade of the rosary. He rattled off the Hail Marys like bullets from a machine gun. One might have expected this to seem too casual or cold, but it was quite the opposite — the familiar words seemed all the more real and authoritative for being recited in such a business-like manner.

We have reliable reports that the rosary was recited in the last moments of the *Titanic,* led by a priest who is himself now a candidate for beatification — Fr. Thomas Byles, an English convert from Protestantism, who chose to stay on the doomed liner despite several opportunities to escape.

Perhaps the saint of modern times who was most dedicated to the rosary was St. Padre Pio of Pietrelcina (1887–1968), the Franciscan priest, friar and mystic. Padre Pio famously called his rosary his

10 Mitch Finley, *The Rosary Handbook: A Guide for Newcomers, Old-Timers and Those in Between* (Ijamsville, Maryland: The Word Among Us Press, 2007), 12.

"weapon" — he would sometimes say to one of his fellow friars "bring me my weapon," meaning his rosary beads. Towards the end of his life, when fellow friars asked him for advice, he would often simply lift up his rosary, wordlessly. Indeed, he rarely took it out of his hands. He would say the rosary up to forty or fifty times a day. When someone asked him how he could manage to say so many rosaries, he replied: "How do you manage not to say any?"

Sister Lucia, the longest-lived Fatima visionary, was even more emphatic: "There is no problem, I tell you, no matter how difficult it is, that we cannot resolve by the prayer of the holy rosary." Remember that Our Lady of Fatima herself asked the children to spread devotion to the rosary. Is the rosary monotonous? St. Josemaría Escrivá had an answer to that: "Blessed be that monotony of Hail Marys, which purifies the monotony of your sins!"

The Rosary is notable for appealing to both the simplest and the most sophisticated believers. St. John Paul II, in the same encyclical in which he proposed the Mysteries of Light, admitted it was his own favorite prayer:

> The rosary is my favorite prayer. A marvellous prayer! Marvellous in its simplicity and its depth.... Against the background of the words *Ave Maria [Hail Mary]* the principal events of the life of Jesus Christ pass before the eyes of the soul. They take shape in the complete series of the joyful, sorrowful and glorious mysteries, and they put us in living communion with Jesus through — we might say — the heart of his Mother. At the same time our heart can embrace in the decades of the rosary all the events that make up the lives of individuals, families, nations, the Church, and all mankind. Our personal concerns and those of our neighbour, especially those who are closest to us, who are dearest to us. Thus the simple prayer of the rosary marks the rhythm of human life.[11]

11 St. John Paul II, *Rosarium Virginis Mariae: On the Most Holy Rosary.* https://w2.vatican.va/content/john-paul-ii/en/apost_letters/2002/documents/hf_jp-ii_apl_20021016_rosarium-virginis-mariae.html (accessed May 28, 2017).

The Pope that was canonized on the very same day as St. John Paul II, St. John XXIII — the Pope who summoned the Second Vatican Council — was equally enthusiastic about the rosary:

> The rosary, which since the beginning of 1953 I have pledged myself to recite devoutly in its entirety, has become an exercise of constant meditation and tranquil daily contemplation, keeping my mind alert in the vast field of my teaching office and my ministry as supreme Pastor of Church and common father of souls.[12]

Some saints have even experienced life-changing inspirations while reciting the rosary. The Italian saint Joseph Cottolengo (1786–1842) was the founder of the Little House of Divine Providence, a refuge for people who were not admitted to hospital for various reasons (such as being infectious). This is one biographer's account of how the idea came to him:

> When St. Joseph was called to the bedside of a dying woman who was refused entry to a general hospital because she was pregnant, and to a maternity hospital because she was sick as well as pregnant, he was haunted that night by the idea of all the sick people who must die without the Last Sacraments. He went to the church as it was about to close, got the sacristan to ring the bell, and led the recitation of the rosary before the altar of Our Lady. Those watching him noticed that, about a third of the way through the rosary, he began to lose his look of anguish, and by the end he looked serene. His eyes lit up with joy at the end, and he said: "The grace has been granted." He had the idea of opening the Pious Institute of the Divine Providence, which began with four beds in a house beside the church, where poor sick people who were waiting to go into hospital could rest.[13]

---

12 St. John XXIII, *Journal of a Soul* (London: A&C Black, 2000), 315.

13 Rev. Henry Louis Hughes, *St. Joseph Cottolengo: The Good Canon* (London: Alexander Ousely Ltd., 1934), 35–36.

At least one saint has died for the Rosary. Blessed Ceferino Giménez Malla was a gypsy who was arrested during the Spanish Revolution for protesting the arrest of a priest. (Contrary to the popular perception of the Spanish Civil War, as promoted by the Abba song "Fernando" and any number of other books, song and films, there were atrocities committed on *both* sides, and hundreds of Catholic martyrs were butchered by left-wing forces.)

Blessed Ceferino Giménez Malla

Blessed Ceferino was taken to a Franciscan monastery which the Republicans were using as a prison. He was told that he would probably be released if he stopped praying the Rosary, but he was not willing to do that. When he was executed, he was holding the Rosary, and he had the words: "Long live Christ the King!" on his lips.

Hopefully, the stories in this chapter will inspire you in your own prayer life. Perhaps this is the most inspiring thought of all; whenever we pray, we can join our prayer to the prayer of all the saints who are now in heaven.

Mirth

St. Philip Neri ✳ St. Miguel Pro ✳ St. Bernadette Soubirous
St. Teresa of Avila ✳ Blessed John Henry Newman
St. John XXIII ✳ St. Maria Mazzerrello

THE CATECHISM OF THE CATHOLIC CHURCH describes "immoderate laughter" as a venial sin, and when we think of saints we rarely think of fun. Indeed, some of the saints seem to have been unrelentingly serious, at least in the accounts that we have of them. It is hard to think of Juniperra Serra, the Spanish missionary to the Americas who would smash a rock against his chest while preaching, cracking a joke. (Though maybe I'm wrong and he did.) However, many of the saints had a vivid sense of humor, and the stories of their lives are not without their amusing moments.

It has often been remarked that Jesus himself, in the gospels, is never portrayed as laughing, or joking. The Mel Gibson movie *The Passion of the Christ* depicts Jesus engaging in some horseplay with his mother, before the beginning of his public ministry, as a contrast with the unrelieved bleakness of most of the movie. However, the Bible itself shows us no such moments. Some have claimed to find humor in some of our Lord's words, under the surface — for instance, in the image of a camel passing through the eye of a needle. I find this unconvincing, and even somewhat trivializing.

G.K. Chesterton wrote a famous passage on this subject, at the very end of his masterpiece *Orthodoxy*:

> And as I close this chaotic volume I open again the strange small book from which all Christianity came; and I am again haunted by a kind of confirmation. The tremendous figure which fills the Gospels towers in this respect, as in every other, above all the

thinkers who ever thought themselves tall. His pathos was natural, almost casual. The Stoics, ancient and modern, were proud of concealing their tears. He never concealed His tears; He showed them plainly on His open face at any daily sight, such as the far sight of His native city. Yet He concealed something. Solemn supermen and imperial diplomatists are proud of restraining their anger. He never restrained His anger. He flung furniture down the front steps of the Temple, and asked men how they expected to escape the damnation of Hell. Yet He restrained something. I say it with reverence; there was in that shattering personality a thread that must be called shyness. There was something that He hid from all men when He went up a mountain to pray. There was something that He covered constantly by abrupt silence or impetuous isolation. There was some one thing that was too great for God to show us when He walked upon our earth; and I have sometimes fancied that it was His mirth.[1]

The saints, on the other hand, have not always concealed their mirth. In fact, there was one saint who famously used mirth to conceal his holiness. St. Philip Neri (died 1595), the founder of the Oratory whom we have already met in an earlier chapter, was famous for his pranks. It seemed as though he wanted to avoid anybody taking too elevated a view of him — such humility is very common amongst the saints.

As his biographer Theodore Maynard tells us:

> It is almost incredible what lengths Philip went to in order to prevent people having a good opinion of him. He would meet the most exalted patronages in fantastic dress, or with his clothes worn inside out, or with large white shoes on his feet. At other times he would strut through the streets in the cloak of marten skins given him by Cardinal Gesualdo to make people think that he was vain of his attire; or he would carry a huge bunch of broom in his hand and stop every now and then, pretending

1 G.K. Chesterton, *Orthodoxy*. http://www.gutenberg.org/cache/epub/130/pg130-images. html (accessed May 28, 2017).

to enjoy the delicious scent. On one occasion he had his beard cut on only one side and went out that way, and tried to draw further attention to himself by dancing. On feast days he was quite likely to show himself in church with a jacket over his cassock and his biretta [ceremonial hat] cocked on one side and with a lay-brother who had been told to keep brushing him off. A large blue cushion was sometimes carried on his head in public. Anything to make people think he was foolish! Nor did his disciples escape having to make themselves ridiculous in the same way…lay brother Giuliano Macaluffi had to perform rustic dances and once was sent into the refectory during supper carrying on his shoulders a monkey holding a gun and wearing a biretta…. One young man was sent out with a placard on his back which read: "For eating curds and whey." Another whose piety led him to ask Philip for permission to wear a hair-shirt, got the permission — but also the injunction to wear the hair-shirt outside his coat, a mortification greater than he had bargained for. As "Berto of the hair-shirt" he was jeered at by all Rome.[2]

On another occasion, after one member of the Oratory had preached a particularly fine sermon, St. Philip asked him to preach it again — six times in a row, word for word. Perhaps the purpose of St. Philip's pranks was not simply to deflect admiration from himself. Perhaps they were an attempt to relate to the people of the day on their own terms — a "New Evangelization" of the sixteenth century.

St. Miguel Pro, the Mexican Jesuit and martyr whom we have met in a previous chapter — you may remember him as the naughty child who bought limitless cakes on his mother's credit — did not lose his sense of fun in later life, despite the danger of being an underground priest at a time when the Catholic Church was persecuted:

Two *tecnicos* [government agents] shadowed him on another occasions, he could feel them close behind him. On turning a

2 Theodore Maynard, *Mystic in Motley: The Life of St. Philip Neri* (Milwaukee: The Bruce Publishing Company, 1946), 180–181.

street corner he perceived a Catholic lady he knew. With a wink he "put her wise," took her arm, and they sauntered off arm in arm. Ten seconds after, the police came into the street—but there was certainly no priest to be seen, only a strolling couple of lovers.

Again, two agents arrived at his house. This time, they thought they had caught something—a big fish! Fr. Pro met them with so much aplomb, such terrible cordiality, and made them laugh so much, that they were convinced they had come on a false scent. To settle the matter he took them off to a café, stood them refreshments, and drank, himself, to their good luck....

It was his obvious duty, and one cannot help seeing it was his pleasure to slip thus dexterously through the fingers of police agents and spies.[3]

It wasn't only in escaping from government agents that his sense of fun showed itself, but also in acts of simple charity:

He might often be seen on the streets of Mexico City with large sacks of provisions on his back...it was a matter of complete indifference to him if the waifs he encountered should laugh at him—he would have laughed louder. On one famous occasion he bore through the streets six chickens and a turkey—all of them alive! Another time he got into a bus with six chickens... and got away with it, as he would have said—he was so genuinely funny he would literally do anything.[4]

St. Bernadette Soubirous, for all her holiness, was a saint who tolerated little nonsense. She was adamant that neither herself nor her family would profit in the smallest way from the fact that Our Blessed Mother had appeared to her. This despite the fact that her family were very poor. Once, when her brother admitted to her that he had received two francs from a lady and gentleman to whom he had shown the

3 Mrs. George Norman, *God's Jester: The Story of the Life and Martyrdom of Fr. Michael Pro* (London: Longman's, Green and Co., 1931), 171.
4 Ibid., 177.

site of the apparitions, St. Bernadette gave him a box in the ear—the soundest he had received in his whole life, he admitted. She also forced him to return the money. There is something irresistibly appealing in the thought of a saint giving her brother a thick ear.

Another saint with a fine sense of humor was Teresa of Avila (died 1582), the Doctor of the Church, mystic, and reformer of monasteries. Although St. Teresa sought to return religious life to its previous austerities, seeing that it had grown lax and indulgent in her time, she was gifted with great common sense. When a fellow sister saw her eating partridge (which had been given to her as a gift) with obvious enjoyment, she asked her whether this was really appropriate of a nun who had taken a vow of penance. "Sister," said St. Teresa, "there is a time for penance and a time for partridge." Another famous story has St. Teresa complaining to Our Blessed Lord after she was badly thrown from a horse. She heard Jesus say to her: "Teresa, whom the Lord loves, he chastises. This is how I treat all my friends." To which the saint replied: "No wonder you have so few!"

A story in which a saint is the occasion rather than the source of the humor involves St. John Neumann (1811–1860), the Czech priest who became Bishop of Philadelphia, whom we have already met. St. Neumann was a gifted linguist, and one of the many languages he mastered was Gaelic. This was so he could hear the confessions of the Irish immigrants to Philadelphia. The story goes that one old woman, after having made her confession and received absolution in Gaelic, said on emerging from the confessional: "Thanks be to God we finally have an Irish bishop!"

Blessed John Henry Newman, the leader of the Oxford Movement mentioned in a previous chapter, was a saint with a keen sense of humor. His novel *Loss and Gain*, which is a thinly fictionalized account of his own conversion, features one wickedly amusing sequence in which a whole succession of visitors come to the protagonist's room. They have heard rumors that he is about to convert, and each one wants him to convert to his or her own particular sect. One lady makes a very surprising offer to him:

Alas, it was a soft, distinct tap at the door; there was no mistake. "Who's there? come in!" he cried; upon which the door gently opened, and a young lady, not without attractions of person and dress, presented herself. Charles started up with vexation; but there was no help for it, and he was obliged to hand her a chair, and then to wait, all expectation, or rather all impatience, to be informed of her mission. For a while she did not speak, but sat, with her head on one side, looking at her parasol, the point of which she fixed on the carpet, while she slowly described a circumference with the handle. At length she asked, without raising her eyes, whether it was true — and she spoke slowly and in what is called a spiritual tone — whether it was true, the information had been given her, that Mr. Reding, the gentleman she had the honour of addressing — whether it was true, that he was in search of a religion more congenial to his feelings than that of the Church of England? "Mr. Reding could not give her any satisfaction on the subject of her inquiry;" — he answered shortly, and had some difficulty in keeping from rudeness in his tone. The interrogation, she went on to say, perhaps might seem impertinent; but she had a motive. Some dear sisters of hers were engaged in organizing a new religious body, and Mr. Reding's accession, counsel, assistance, would be particularly valuable; the more so, because as yet they had not any gentleman of University education among them.

"May I ask," said Charles, "the name of the intended persuasion?"

"The name," she answered, "is not fixed; indeed, this is one of the points on which we should covet the privilege of the advice of a gentleman so well qualified as Mr. Reding to assist us in our deliberations."

"And your tenets, ma'am?"

"Here, too," she replied, "there is much still to be done; the tenets are not fixed either, that is, they are but sketched; and we shall prize your suggestions much. Nay, you will of course have the opportunity, as you would have the right to nominate any doctrine to which you may be especially inclined."

Charles did not know how to answer to so liberal an offer.[5]

One story has it that, when Blessed Newman was asked for his views on the role of the laity (that is, Christians who are not priests, religious sisters, or religious brothers), he replied: "Well, we'd look rather silly without them, wouldn't we?"

You may be surprised to hear that St. Padre Pio, the "victim soul" who endured so much suffering and who appears so earnest in most of his photographs, was quite fond of jokes. His favorite joke has been retold in so many different versions that it is hard to tell which version he told himself. But it goes something like this:

> When trains were a new thing in Italy, a farmer who had never traveled on one before purchased a ticket to see his daughter in another town. The clerk in the ticket office sold him a return ticket to her town, explaining that it entitled him to a journey there and a journey back. When the train entered a long, dark tunnel, the farmer cried in surprise: "Where are we going?" A fellow passenger, deciding to have some fun with such an obvious "hick," replied: "We are going to Hell." "Well, I'm not worried," said the farmer, complacently. "I have a return ticket."

Jokes about hell might be considered surprising coming from a saint, but it's not the only example of this. I've already mentioned Blessed John Sullivan, the Irish Jesuit who converted from Protestantism and who was known as "the saint on a bike." Despite his usually melancholy disposition, he occasionally told jokes, some of them about his former denomination:

> There was one story on the subject of Hell which seems to me now to be almost too good to be true, though my recollection is

5 Blessed John Henry Newman, *Loss and Gain*. http://www.newmanreader.org/works/gain/chapter3-7.html (accessed May 28, 2017).

that he assured us the incident actually occurred.

A clergyman was preaching on Hell, and assured his hearers that, though many seemed to doubt of its existence, he had no doubt whatsoever, since he had met people so wicked and base that there was no other place suitable for them. Then in a burst of confidence he added: "I may as well tell you that I firmly believe that an aunt of mine is in Hell."

This was too much for one of the congregation, who got up and began to go out.

"Look at that man," exclaimed the clergyman. "He won't believe my words, but he is headed straight for Hell."

The erring sheep was at the door, but at this time he turned round.

"Have you any message for your aunt, sir?" he enquired politely.[6]

Even saints who have occupied the august office of Pope have occasionally enjoyed a bit of fun. I like this story of St. Pius X (died 1914):

Every first Communicant in Rome was invited to the Vatican and Pope Pius would give them short instructions.

Once, the Pope teased a little boy by asking him his name, which was Giulio.

The boy had long curls, which the Pope ran through his fingers, and replied: "What a pretty name, Giulia."

"It is not Giulia, it is Giulio," the boy said.

"It is really a pretty name — Giulia," the Pope repeated.

"Can't you see I'm not a little girl?" asked the boy, pulling up his tunic. "Don't you see I have knickers on?"[7]

("Knickers" in this context are "knickerbockers," a kind of baggy trousers for men and boys.)

6 Fergal McGrath S.J., *Father John Sullivan S.J.* (London: Longman's, Green and Co., 1941), 79.

7 Katherine Burton, *The Great Mantle: The Life of Giuseppe Melchiore Sarto, Pope Pius X* (London: Longman's, Green, 1950), 91.

St. John XXIII (died 1963) is another Pope-saint who was well-known for his sense of humour, and his witticisms have been told and retold. Like Pope Pius X, he was from a very humble background, and he once reportedly made this quip about his family's economic woes: "There are three ways to face ruin: women, gambling and farming. My father chose the most boring one." Another witticism attributed to him is: "It often happens that I wake up at night and begin to think about the serious problems afflicting the world and I tell myself, I must talk to the Pope about it. Then the next day when I wake up I remember that I am the Pope."

Here is a story of saintly humor in the face of death itself. St. Maria Mazzerrello (1837–1881) was the founder of the Salesian Sisters, a religious order dedicated to providing education and vocational training to disadvantaged girls. She worked alongside St. John Bosco, who did similar work amongst boys. St. Maria Mazzerrello died of a fever after she and her fellow sisters were forced to sleep in the open air, on account of a mix-up regarding their lodging, when they were en route to some members of their order in France. When she was given the last rites, she said to the priest: "Now that I've got my passport, have I permission to leave?"[8]

Which brings us nicely to the next chapter…

---

8   Ann Ball, *Modern Saints: Their Lives and Faces: Book One* (1983), 83.

Death

St. Louis-Marie Grignion de Montfort
St. Louise de Marillac ✳ St. Robert Southwell
St. Joseph Pignatelli ✳ St. John Berchmans
St. Oliver Plunkett ✳ St. Miguel Pro
St. Bernadette Soubirous ✳ St. Josemaría Escrivá
St. Gemma Galgani ✳ St. John Paul II
St. Elizabeth of the Trinity

IF THERE IS ONE SUBJECT THAT SHOWS THE DIF-
ference between Christian and secular society, it is the subject of
death. Although many (perhaps most) people in post-Christian society
continue to believe in some kind of afterlife — very often described as
the "Great Such-and-Such in the Sky" (replace "Such-and-Such" with
whatever is appropriate to the deceased person) — more and more
people seem to accept that death is simply annihilation. "The lights
go out, that's it," as one character in the 2010 movie *Hereafter* says.

Most people who expect annihilation after death don't seem to be
particularly upset at the prospect. While some famous figures such as
Samuel Johnson (poet, wit and writer of the first English dictionary)
and Philip Larkin (poet and librarian) have eloquently described their
terror at the prospect of nothingness, the majority of people who
expect this seem to take it in their stride. And, indeed, it has often
been pointed out that the dread of non-existence is entirely irrational.
"I was perfectly content before I was born, and I think of death as the
same state," said film critic Roger Ebert, shortly before his own death.

I have attended a couple of humanist funerals, and I must admit
they were carried off with considerable dignity. In both cases, they
were a celebration of the person's life. Prayers and Scripture readings
were replaced by the deceased's favorite songs and poems. Perhaps this

is more personal and modest, but it certainly lacked the sense of awe that we experience at Christian funerals. It's no surprise that humanist funerals focus on life rather than death. What is there, from the point of view of those who believe in annihilation, to say about death itself? It is literally nothing, a void. For this reason, contemporary society has very little to say about death *as such*. We speak about mortality, but that is something different. That is the frame around life, the ticking clock that tells us to make the most of our days. Death itself (as a popular funeral reading puts it, though in a completely different sense) is "nothing at all."

For Christians, and for Christian societies, death is something very different. It is terrible, because it is the moment when our eternal destiny is decided; Heaven or Hell. (We may go to Purgatory, but in that case we are still destined for Heaven.) In the life of a saint, it is the culminating moment of triumph, the moment in which the saint is told to "enter into the joy of your master" (Matthew 25:23). Christian religious art tends to emphasize death, rather than avoiding it. Many pictures of saints feature a skull, as a *memento mori* (which means "reminder of death"). Very often the saint is contemplating the skull.

St. Bernadette

As well as this, the bodies of Catholic saints (both incorrupt, and in pictures taken immediately after death) have a serene beauty about them which makes death seem a glorious culmination rather than a full stop. How beautiful St. Bernadette looks in the repose of death! We are reminded of the words of St. Paul at the end of his life: "I have fought the good fight, I have finished the race, I have kept the faith" (2 Timothy 4:7).

While secular society may encourage us to think about our mortality, in order to squeeze the last drop of juice from life before it is over, Christianity has traditionally encouraged us to think about *death itself*. More specifically, it has encouraged us to think of the "four last things": death, judgment, Heaven and Hell. A prayer that many Catholics say every day, the Hail Mary, ends with the line: "Pray for us sinners now and at the hour of our death."

One saint who excelled in making his listeners contemplate death was St. Louis-Marie Grignion de Montfort (1673–1716), a priest, preacher, and writer of celebrated spiritual works on Mary and the rosary:

> De Montfort excelled in his triduums on the preparation for death. For three days he would speak to his listeners of their last end; how that he must die, that death is near, uncertain, terrible; how much the death of the sinner is to be dreaded, and that of the just to be desired; that we die as we have lived. On the third day there was corporate Communion, for which each must prepare as if it were his last. A strange scene towards evening would crown this retreat, of which the missioner had made a drama. Montfort seated on a chair in the midst of the church, would play the part of a dying man. Two of his helpers would be near, the one the Good Angel, the other the Tempter. And they would fight for this soul which was about to appear before God, the devil trying to discourage him by reminding him of his faults, the angel urging him to contrition, and exhorting him to invoke the divine mercy. A medieval mystery indeed![1]

However, even drawing the attention of sinners to their last end can be done in a clumsy way, as St. Louise de Marillac (1591–1660), who co-founded the Sisters of Charity with St. Vincent de Paul, realized:

1 George Rigault, *Blessed Louis-Marie Grignion de Montfort; His Life and Work* (London: Burns and Oates and Washbourne, 1932), 120.

Members of her order had been known to "fatigue and harass" the dying by excessive talking when visiting, to which St. Louise said: "Please remember to warn the ladies not to speak at great length to those in grave danger. It would be wise in the case of those who had not made their general confessions to warn them of the necessity of accusing themselves of sins which they had either held back and forgotten in previous confessions, with the good will and intention of accusing themselves of all sins committed against God and neighbour. Also if possible to encourage them to make short acts of faith, hope and charity."[2]

In his book *The Triumphs over Death*, the English Jesuit, poet and martyr St. Robert Southwell (1561–1595), who was to be publicly hanged at a time of Catholic persecution in England, had consoling words for those who had lost their loved ones:

> It could not displease you to see your friend removed out of a ruinous house, and the house destroyed, and pulled down, if you knew it were to built in a statelier form, and to transfer the inhabitant with more joy into a fairer lodging. Let then your sister's soul depart without grief; let her body also be altered into dust; withdraw your eyes from the ruin of this cottage, and cast them upon the majesty of the second building, which St. Paul saith shall be incorruptible, glorious, strange, spiritual and immortal.[3]

Saints have also been foremost in comforting and accompanying the dying themselves. St. Joseph Pignatelli (1737–1811) was a Spanish priest, a Jesuit when it was very unpopular to be a Jesuit. Governments all over Europe were banning the Jesuits from their realms, since they were seen as trouble-makers, and since government coveted their significant financial interests. Eventually the Pope himself, spurred on by political

2 Lady Alice Lovatt, *Life of the Venerable Louise de Marillac (Mademoiselle de Gras), Foundress of the Company of Sisters of Charity of St. Vincent de Paul* (1916), 105.

3 St. Robert Southwell, *The Triumphs Over Death; or, a Consolatory Epistle for Afflicted Minds, in the Affects of Dying Friends* (London: Simpkin, Marshall, Hamilton, Kent, and Co., 1814), 15.

rulers, suppressed them. When they were driven to non-Catholic countries such as Russia, St. Pignatelli acted as their leader, and when the suppression was lifted he helped to re-establish them. In his early days as a priest, however, he worked as a prison chaplain, and part of his duties was to accompany prisoners condemned to execution:

> From the moment the prisoner entered his cell to the moment of his death, Fr. Pignatelli gave much of his time to be with him. He sat beside him on the stone bench of his cell and conversed with him as a friend. With soft, gentle words he spoke to him of the wickedness of sin and the justice of its punishment; of the reckoning all must make to God of their lives, of the mercy of God; of Christ's atoning sacrifice on the Cross and the love of the Sacred Heart for sinners. It was exceptional if he did not succeed in having the man make his peace with God, then brought him the Blessed Sacrament, and thus prepared him to meet his Maker. He always accomplished the doomed man from the jail to the gallows, and stood beside him when he fell.[4]

What is especially interesting in this account is that St. Pignatelli did not see his role as simply to "walk with" the condemned prisoner, but also to convince him of his need for repentance in his final moments — even to convince him of "the justice of his punishment." Today, when so many Catholics are stridently opposed to the death penalty, this seems strange and harsh. But here, as so often, we see that the saints are not mere humanitarians, but always have the *supernatural* good of others in the forefront of their minds, rather than the merely natural good. Death is not the worst thing that can happen to us.

I have several times mentioned the short-lived Jesuit saint, St. John Berchmans. Did this saint regret the shortness of his days, dying at the age of twenty-two? On the contrary, he had wanted to become an army chaplain, in the hope of becoming a martyr. This is how he received the news of his imminent death, when it came:

---

4 Monsignor D.A. Hanly, *Blessed Joseph Pignatelli of the Society of Jesus: A Great Hero in a Great Crisis* (New York: Benziger Brothers, 1937), 44.

John said gaily: "Come, Brother, let us prepare ourselves. I assure you that you could not have given me any news that could be more agreeable, and that you could not have given me any greater pleasure." And grasping his crucifix he said: "Dear Lord, behold all that I possess, and all that I have possessed in this life! Therefore do not abandon me, my good Jesus." The infirmarian became more and more moved, and recommended himself to John's prayers, and at the same time felt it his duty to beg John to moderate the ardor which was exhausting his strength. John replied that nothing did more good to his own soul.[5]

As with many saints, the last words of St. John were the names "Mary and Jesus."

When it comes to the deaths of saints themselves, it would be easy to fill this entire book with inspiring tales of their last moments. Perhaps the most compelling of such stories are the deaths of Christian martyrs. "The blood of the martyrs is the seed of the Church" runs one ancient saying, and the twentieth century gave us hundreds of new martyrs, victims of the Nazis, the communists, and other anti-Catholic regimes. Indeed, the rise of radical Islam in our own time makes it possible that Christian martyrdom will once again become a reality in the Western world. The murder of Fr. Jacques Hamel by young Islamic radicals, while he was celebrating Mass, shocked the world on the 26th of July 2016. His cause for canonization has already been opened.

I would like to go back a few centuries, though, to the last Irish person to be declared a saint — St. Oliver Plunkett, the Catholic Primate of All Ireland, who was martyred in 1681. He was the last victim of the Popish Plot, an anti-Catholic hysteria which was fueled by a sadistic opportunist called Titus Oates. Oates convinced many of the English that Catholics were plotting to kill King Charles II and replace him with his (Catholic) brother James.

Considering that he is the last Catholic martyr in England, and the last Irish person to be declared a saint, there is remarkably little fuss

---

5 Hippolyte Delehaye, *St. John Berchmans* (New York: Benziger Brothers, 1921), 155.

about St. Oliver Plunkett in his native land—even amongst Catholics. In fact, in his book *The Saints and Martyrs of Ireland*, H. Patrick Montague writes:

> In his case…there were serious limitations to the strength of the veneration which is so evident in the case of many of the traditional saints. Oliver Plunkett was never fully accepted as one of the native Irish, a fact of supreme importance in his time. It took three hundred years before a miracle, not in Ireland but in an Italian hospital, finally decided the issue of his canonisation.[6]

Why should St. Oliver Plunkett, born in Ireland as he was, not be considered "one of the native Irish"? Because, as with so many English and Catholic priests of his era, he received his priestly formation in Rome. At this time, Irish Catholicism, as well as being suppressed by the state, was riven by geographical and cultural divisions. Different factions lobbied to have their own candidate ordained as Archbishop of Armagh, the head of the Catholic Church in Ireland. The Pope decided to ignore them all and make Plunkett, who was a professor of theology in Rome, the Archbishop. Naturally, this did not go down well in Ireland.

When he reached Ireland, St. Oliver often had to be a stern father to his flock. The wars and ethnic displacement that Oliver Cromwell, Lord Protector of England and scourge of Catholics, had recently inflicted on the country had left the Irish Catholic Church in chaos. Drunkenness, money-grabbing and even sexual immorality were rife in the demoralized Irish priesthood, and St. Oliver clamped down hard on them. As well as this, St. Oliver's personality was—as his biographer Desmond Forristal has pointed out—somewhat austere and aristocratic, hardly fitting him for the role of a folk hero.

But if Oliver Plunkett never really kindled the imagination of the Irish, he soon won their respect with his piety, his integrity, and his energy—he confirmed tens of thousands of people who had not had

---

6 H. Patrick Montague, *The Saints and Martyrs of Ireland* (Gerrards Cross: Colin Smythe, 1981), 90.

access to the sacrament of confirmation during Oliver Cromwell's persecution. Even the Protestant clergy and aristocracy came to respect him. So when an allegation was made that St. Oliver was part of the mythical Popish Plot — he was accused of conspiring in a planned French invasion of Ireland — a jury of Irish Protestants was unwilling to convict him, and his case was moved to England, where it was conducted in farcical conditions.

Brought to Newgate Prison, St. Oliver prepared most seriously for death. One of his fellow prisoners, the English Benedictine priest Fr. Maurus Corker, wrote: "He spent his time in almost continuous prayer…he fasted usually three or four days a week with nothing but bread…he appeared to them always modestly cheerful, without any anguish or concern at his danger or strict confinement, that by his sweet and pious demeanor he attracted an esteem and reverence from those few that came near him."[7]

There is something very impressive in the spectacle of a man who expects to be martyred for his Faith spending his last weeks in such austerity. In such a situation, many of us would be inclined to make the most of whatever innocent worldly pleasures were still available to us, or at least to go easy on ourselves. That even these circumstances were not sufficient to draw St. Oliver away from his calm and disciplined manner of life is perhaps the most endearing part of his story. The Father Corker quoted above was in fact allowed to hear St. Oliver's confessions towards the very end, and the Archbishop placed himself completely under the other priest's authority:

> After he certainly knew God Almighty had chosen him to the crown and dignity of martyrdom, he continually studied how to divest himself of himself, and become more and more an entire pleasing and perfect holocaust…about an hour before he was carried to execution, being desired [asked] to drink a little glass of sack to strengthen his spirits, he answered he was not at his own disposal but mine, and that he must have leave from me

7 Desmond Forristal, "St. Oliver Plunkett." *The Furrow*, Vol. 38 No. 2 (1987), 89–96.

before he would either take it or refuse it...whereupon, though I was locked up, yet for his satisfaction the man and his keeper's wife came to my chamber, and then coming back told him I enjoined it, upon which he readily submitted.[8]

Archbishop Plunkett was hanged at London's famous Tyburn gallows, protesting his innocence of any conspiracy and forgiving his enemies in his final speech. Few people, if any, believed that he was actually guilty of treason, but the judge who condemned him had told him: "The bottom of your treason was your setting up your false religion, than which there is not anything more displeasing to God, or more pernicious to mankind in the world." In other words, St. Oliver Plunkett was executed for being a Catholic.

Let us leap forward almost three centuries, and return to the story of Miguel Pro, the Mexican Jesuit who flamboyantly evaded capture by an anti-Catholic government through disguises and audacity, and who once carried six chickens onto a bus, destined for needy recipients. In November 1927, St. Miguel Pro was finally captured, along with two of his brothers, and two others. He was sentenced to death for a supposed assassination attempt on the life of the anti-Catholic President, Plutarco Elias Calles. There was no trial, and Fr. Miguel and the others were not even told that they had been sentenced to execution, although they guessed it. As he was led out to be shot, Fr. Miguel told his executioners that he forgave them, and his last request was a brief period of time to kneel and pray.

President Calles had invited photographers to the execution, believing either that the men would cower in the face of death, or simply that the pictures of their executions would intimidate Catholics who were rebelling against his government. We can thank President Calles for perhaps the most remarkable photograph ever taken of a Catholic martyr; St. Miguel Pro calmly extending his arms like Christ upon the Cross. Witnesses record that his last words were: "Viva Cristo Rey!" (Long Live Christ the King!)

8 Ibid., 95–96.

St. Miguel Pro

Given the dramatic nature of his martyrdom — indeed, given the romance of his life as a whole — it is extraordinary that St. Miguel Pro is virtually unknown to the general public. I have included his story here, along with the story of St. Oliver Plunkett, as I believe they are both inspiring tales which deserve to be more widely known.

There are an abundance of other enthralling tales of martyrdom throughout Catholic history. I have already described the martyrdom of St. Maximilian Kolbe, who voluntarily took the place of a man sentenced to death in Auschwitz extermination camp. St. Edith Stein's martyrdom in the same camp is also well known. There are any number of others. It is unlikely that you or I will ever face the prospect of martyrdom. But the courage of Catholic martyrs can inspire us to be more courageous in speaking up for the Faith, and in living up to its sometimes difficult demands. As the Letter to the Hebrews tell us: "In the fight against sin, you have not yet had to keep fighting to the point of bloodshed" (Hebrews 12:4).

Of course, martyrdom is not the only form of holy death. St. Gemma Galgani, the Italian mystic mentioned often before in these pages, died on Holy Saturday of 1903, after passing through a final ecstasy on Good Friday which one witness described as similar to that of Jesus dying on the Cross. Gemma reported that the Devil, who had assaulted her throughout her life, made ferocious efforts to drive her to despair. At one point he took the form of a serpent wrapping himself around her. It is fitting that the name of Jesus, which occurs constantly in the letters of St. Gemma, should have been her last word in this world: "Now it is indeed true that nothing more remains to me, Jesus. I recommend my poor soul to Thee…Jesus!" After all St. Gemma's sufferings, she died with a heavenly smile on her lips.

A saint's death that held the world spellbound was the death of St. John Paul II, which occurred on April 2ⁿᵈ 2005. The increasingly frail Pope had just recovered from a bout of flu and an operation on his throat. He developed septic shock from a urinary tract infection, and in his last days struggled to breathe and to speak. But he retained consciousness until he slipped into a coma a few hours before his death. He died in his private residence in the Vatican, while friends surrounded him and thousands of well-wishers gathered in St. Peter's Square. In his final hours he asked to have the Bible read to him. Nine chapters from the gospel of John were read. He had Mass celebrated in his room, and spoke these final words in Polish: "Allow me to depart to the house of the Father."

The deaths of many saints are less picturesque. St. Josemaría Escrivá, who I have mentioned so often, collapsed in the office of a fellow priest, his last words being: "I don't feel well." St. Bernadette Soubirous died of tuberculosis, on Easter Wednesday, at the age of thirty-five. Her final illness had been a long one. Her last words seem to have been "I am thirsty." After drinking the glass of water she was given, she blessed herself and passed away.

It seems appropriate that the last saint I should mention is amongst the very latest to be canonized at the time of writing—St. Elizabeth of the Trinity (1880–1906), the Spanish Carmelite contemplative who was declared a saint by Pope Francis in October 2016, along with seven others. I have mentioned her already, in my chapter on childhood—her mother predicted that she would be either a terror or a saint. St. Elizabeth was an outgoing young woman who enjoyed dancing and had serious gifts as a musician, but she was drawn to the contemplative life. She wished to become a Carmelite, but deferred to her mother's wish to wait until she was twenty-one. When she entered the convent, she only had five years of life remaining to her. She is celebrated for her writings on prayer—a prayer to the Trinity which she wrote is reproduced in the *Catechism of the Catholic Church*. She emphasized the indwelling of the Trinity in the soul of every baptized person, and her spirituality is marked by a radical simplicity.

In an edition of the magazine *Carmel* released at the time of her beatification in 1984, Philip Boyce OCD wrote about the day on which St. Elizabeth professed her final vows:

St. Elizabeth of the Trinity

That profession day was to a certain extent the definitive day of her life, a day that would last into eternity. In a sense, the day that ended for her the weary beat of time and condensed the remaining days of her life into the rhythm of eternity. She expressed this thought more than once at the time of her commitment [to religious life]. Just before profession she wrote: "I would like it to be the beginning of an act of adoration that will never end in my soul." And immediately afterwards: "...profession, it is a day without sunset. I think it is already like the beginning of the day that never ends."[9]

The last eight months of St. Elizabeth's life have been described as a "true Calvary," as she died a lingering death of Addison's disease. This is a disease of the adrenal glands which, in St. Elizabeth's time, had no cure. Amongst other symptoms, the afflicted person had trouble eating and would waste away. On All Saints' Day of 1906, her fellow Carmelites believed that she was passing away, but she rallied. On that day, she said to them: "Everything passes away! At the evening of life, love alone remains." Some days later, after she had been suffering particularly badly, she said: "O love, Love! You know if I love you, if I desire to contemplate you; you know, too, if I suffer; yet, thirty, forty years more if you wish, I am ready." Her last words before she died were: "I am going to light, to love, to life!"

Like all the saints in this chapter—like all the saints in this book—she had entered into the day without sunset, the day that never ends.

---

9 Philip Boyce OCD, "Response and Surrender: The Religious Profession of Blessed Elizabeth of the Trinity." *Mount Carmel: A Quarterly Review of the Religious Life* (1984), 188.

Afterword

LET US AGAIN CONTEMPLATE THE PASSAGE FROM
the Book of Apocalypse with which I began this book, which is read
from the altar on All Saints' Day:

> After this I had a vision of a great multitude,
> which no one could count,
> from every nation, race, people, and tongue.
> They stood before the throne and before the Lamb,
> wearing white robes and holding palm branches in their hands.
> They cried out in a loud voice:
> "Salvation comes from our God, who is seated on the throne,
> and from the Lamb."

The history of the Catholic Church is the greatest love story ever
told. The saints were lovers, consumed by the love of Christ. They
beckon us to emulate that love. "Follow my example, as I follow the
example of Christ" (1 Corinthians 11:1).

"I have come to bring fire to the earth," said Jesus. Such a fire burned
in the hearts of saints, and in their lives, and in their words. My hope
is that some of this fire emanates from the pages of this book, too.

Viva Cristo Rey! Long reign Jesus Christ the King!

Appendix

G.K. Chesterton, Servant of God

Servant of God, G.K. Chesterton

IN THIS BOOK, AS I HAVE PREVIOUSLY EXPLAINED, I wanted to include only people whom we *know* are in Heaven; that is, men and women who have been either beatified or canonized by the Church. It was difficult to leave out so many figures who I admire greatly, particularly Irish people on the road to sainthood; such as

Servant of God Frank Duff, founder of the Legion of Mary (the biggest lay association in the Catholic Church); Edel Quinn, a Legion of Mary missionary who spread the Legion of Mary through Africa; and Venerable Matt Talbot, a Dublin man who overcame extreme alcoholism and thenceforth lived a life of extreme holiness. These and many others have inspired me in my own Christian faith.

However, there is one figure I feel compelled to add, who has not yet even attained the title of Venerable, though his cause for sainthood was opened in 2014. That is Gilbert Keith Chesterton, the English journalist, novelist, poet, wit, and Catholic convert, who died in 1936.

It was Chesterton's writings, more than anything else, which led me to accept the truth of the Catholic faith. And he didn't have this effect just on me; since his own reception into the Church in 1922, Chesterton has drawn a huge number of people along with him. Not only that, but his writings have provided them with powerful ammunition in debates against the Church's many opponents. Chesterton sends us into battle, not only with determination, but with a certain joyous exuberance.

If Chesterton was indeed a saint, he's something of an unusual saint; an enormously fat man, who was notoriously untidy and disheveled, and very fond of spending time in pubs. He didn't seem tremendously enthusiastic about church-going, either; as an Anglican, he rarely seemed to go to church at all. As a Catholic, he fulfilled his Sunday and holy day obligations, but he seems to have rarely gone to Mass other than that. He went to confession once a year, when his wife pushed him to it. It is said that his loud confession was audible in the nearby pews.

On the other hand, Christ was never far from his thoughts. He would make the sign of the Cross with his match before lighting a cigar. He claimed (perhaps metaphorically) that he said grace before dipping his pen in ink. He wrote about every subject under the sun, but he nearly always found a way to bring Christianity into the discussion; not in a contrived way, but simply because his outlook was so essentially Christian. Bear in mind that Chesterton was usually writing for a secular audience, one that was largely Protestant or agnostic.

He could entertain them and evangelize them at the same time. He got away with evangelizing because he was so entertaining. George Orwell complained that, in the last twenty years of his life, Chesterton's writing became "an endless repetition of the same thing"—Catholic propaganda, in Orwell's view. Although Orwell is here betraying his sourness towards Catholicism, and although Chesterton's writing was never monotonous, there is an element of truth to his claim. Chesterton never stopped proclaiming the truth of the Catholic faith.

Is Chesterton in Heaven? It is hard for many of us to believe otherwise. Even those who were his ideological opponents had a warm regard for him, often a love for him. Rarely did he make a bad impression on anybody; and as we have seen, being a saint is no guarantee whatsoever that you are going to be universally liked. He also drew untold numbers of people into the Catholic Church, through the many books and articles in which he argued for the truth of the Catholic faith. There seems to have been no element of malice, cruelty, or egotism in his personality. The worst criticism of his personal behavior that I've encountered is that he tended to get cranky whenever anyone (usually his wife) tried to keep him to a schedule or impose any kind of discipline on him.

His good humor was so legendary that there are only a handful of anecdotes in which he seems to have lost it. When his friend Fr. John O'Connor (the model for Chesterton's fictional detective Father Brown) offered the obese Chesterton his arm when crossing a field, Chesterton refused it "with a finality foreign to our friendship." He then slipped and broke his arm. In another story, Chesterton ordered a child—one of the many children who visited his home—to go up to her bedroom because she had insulted a servant. This was so out of character that it merits a mention in his biography! Finally, a friend of Chesterton recalls that he slammed a bottle down on the table in annoyance when she dilly-dallied about whether or not she would like a glass of wine. Reader, can you imagine if these were the *worst* stories told about you?

In order to be declared venerable, a candidate for sainthood must be judged to have lived the Christian virtues to a heroic degree; that is, the theological virtues of faith, hope and charity, and the cardinal virtues of prudence, justice, fortitude, and temperance. Whether Chesterton, that very fat man, was distinguished for the virtue of temperance may be questioned (and has been questioned). However, it would be hard to argue that he did not live out the virtue of fortitude. Few writers have worked so hard. He wrote over a hundred books and over *four thousand essays*. This is to say nothing of his contributions to other people's books, or the many lectures he gave.

None of this was because Chesterton was a compulsive writer. He wrote to defend the things he believed in, as well as simply to make money. He had to make lots of money, because he gave money away as fast as he could make it. A lot of the money he made was given directly to people who asked him for charity — he was a notorious "soft touch." Another beneficiary was an organization dear to his heart: the Distributist League. Distributism was an organized attempt to apply the social teachings of Leo XIII and subsequent popes. It was an attempt to create an alternative to both socialism and the sort of capitalism by which massive companies squeezed out small businesses, small shops, and small farms. How far Distributism actually reflects the social teaching of the Church is a matter for debate; how far it succeeded is also a matter for debate. It seems to have had little tangible success. Yet it cannot be denied that Chesterton made titanic efforts in championing a cause he believed in, one which he also believed to be an application of Catholic ideals to economic and social life. Ultimately, only God knows the degree to which our efforts fail or succeed.

As I say, only the Church can decide whether Chesterton was a saint or not. But he certainly possesses one of the traits which seems characteristic of the saints, and which I have tried to highlight in this book; that is, the ability to make virtue attractive, and to make vice ugly. This is the opposite of so many modern celebrities, who have a tendency to do just the opposite.

Chesterton makes virtue attractive through his writing. After reading one of Chesterton's books, the reader feels *excited* to pursue the Christian ideal; he makes it seem almost like a romp or a sport.

An example is this celebration of family life, from his book *Heretics*:

This is, indeed, the sublime and special romance of the family. It is romantic because it is a toss-up. It is romantic because it is everything that its enemies call it. It is romantic because it is arbitrary. It is romantic because it is there. So long as you have groups of men chosen rationally, you have some special or sectarian atmosphere. It is when you have groups of men chosen irrationally that you have men. The element of adventure begins to exist; for an adventure is, by its nature, a thing that comes to us. It is a thing that chooses us, not a thing that we choose. The supreme adventure is being born. There we do walk suddenly into a splendid and startling trap. There we do see something of which we have not dreamed before. Our father and mother do lie in wait for us and leap out on us, like brigands from a bush. Our uncle is a surprise. Our aunt is, in the beautiful common expression, a bolt from the blue. When we step into the family, by the act of being born, we do step into a world which is incalculable, into a world which has its own strange laws, into a world which could do without us, into a world that we have not made. In other words, when we step into the family we step into a fairy-tale.[1]

How many writers could make all the irritations and vexations of family life seem exciting, even romantic, as Chesterton does here?

Another example of Chesterton making virtue seem attractive, even fun, is his defense of humility in *The Defendant*:

Humility is the luxurious art of reducing ourselves to a point, not to a small thing or a large one, but to a thing with no size at all, so that to it all the cosmic things are what they really are — of immeasurable stature. That the trees are high and the grasses short is a mere accident of our own foot-rules and our own stature. But to the spirit which has stripped off for a moment its own idle temporal standards the grass is an everlasting forest, with dragons for denizens; the stones of the road are as incredible mountains

1 G.K. Chesterton, *Heretics*, http://gutenberg.net.au/ebooks09/0900611.txt (accessed January 26, 2018).

piled one upon the other; the dandelions are like gigantic bonfires illuminating the lands around; and the heath-bells on their stalks are like planets hung in heaven each higher than the other. Between one stake of a paling and another there are new and terrible landscapes; here a desert, with nothing but one misshapen rock; here a miraculous forest, of which all the trees flower above the head with the hues of sunset; here, again, a sea full of monsters that Dante would not have dared to dream. These are the visions of him who, like the child in the fairy tales, is not afraid to become small.[2]

The reader of Chesterton who learns something of the man's life will also be inspired by the knowledge that Chesterton *lived* the Christian ideal. His humility shines through his writings. But we also know from the accounts of his life that he *was* profoundly humble. For instance, he would often give people signed copies of his books; in such cases, he was always apologetic and embarrassed that he had nothing better to give them, and it seems clear that this was genuine humility and not a pretense. Although his career brought him into contact with many famous men, he was no less interested in the barbers who cut his hair and the cab drivers who took him from place to place, and many of them have left touching accounts of him — Chesterton, they said, made *them* feel interesting and important.

Another instance in which Chesterton's example is as moving as his writing is his love for his wife. He was never naïve about marriage or the family; he once described marriage as a duel to the death which no man of honor should refuse, and he wasn't entirely joking. But, by all accounts, he loved his wife passionately to the moment of his death.

I will mention one more Christian virtue that Chesterton showed in his life; that is, obedience to Christ's commandment to love our enemies. In his long career, Chesterton debated many of the leading intellects of the day. Very often, he was in passionate disagreement with them. But he never let disagreement lead to unpleasantness. Indeed, he joked that the worst thing about a quarrel was that it ruined an argument.

2 G.K. Chesterton, *The Defendant*, http://www.gutenberg.org/files/12245/12245-h/12245-h. htm (accessed January 26, 2018).

Chesterton was so good-humored in debate that, not only did he love his enemies, his enemies loved him! George Bernard Shaw was one example. The two men were engaged in constant public debates, often on very fundamental matters. Yet they were good friends.

So we know that Chesterton lived the virtues he wrote about; but it is in his writings that we will encounter it most vividly today. And what charms generation after generation of reader is the *simple goodness* that radiates from his writings. One biography of Chesterton is entitled *Wisdom and Innocence*, and the phrase "innocence" naturally comes to mind when Chesterton is discussed. One can read through all his books and find nothing that is sexually suggestive, nothing that is scatological, nothing that is cynical, nothing that is crass, nothing that is morbid. To read Chesterton is to breathe fresh air—and your lungs cry out for more. The reader of Chesterton wishes, not only to read more Chesterton, but to emulate him.

If there is one word that is applied to Chesterton even more often than "innocence," it is "wonder." In all his writing, he sought to awaken his readers to the wonder of existence itself: "We live in the best of all impossible worlds." And wonder leads us to gratitude. As a young man, before he had even become a Christian, he wrote a short poem in which this sense of grateful wonder is expressed unforgettably:

> Here dies another day
> During which I have had eyes, ears, hands,
> And the great world around me;
> And with tomorrow begins another.
> Why am I allowed two?

Most importantly of all, G.K. Chesterton draws us to Christ. Not only have Chesterton's works been responsible for innumerable conversions to Christianity, but they have stoked the flame of faith in those who were already Christians. In this, at least, he resembles the saints that fill the pages of this book. If you have never read him, reader, I urge you to put down this book and pick up the first Chesterton book you can find!

ABOUT THE AUTHOR

MAOLSHEACHLANN Ó CEALLAIGH WAS
born in Dublin in 1977 and has worked in the library of
University College Dublin since 2001. He has written for
such publications as *The Irish Catholic*, *The Catholic Voice*,
Ireland's Own, *Annals Australasia*, *Spirituality*, and *Books
Ireland*, as well as for *Sunday Miscellany* on RTE radio.
He writes a weekly column on G.K. Chesterton for *The
Open Door* magazine, and his blog *Irish Papist* has been
online since 2011.

CPSIA information can be obtained
at www.ICGtesting.com
Printed in the USA
FSHW010213240919
62315FS